Modern API Design with ASP.NET Core 2

Building Cross-Platform Back-End Systems

Fanie Reynders

Foreword by Scott Hanselman

Apress®

Modern API Design with ASP.NET Core 2: Building Cross-Platform Back-End Systems

Fanie Reynders
Odijk, The Netherlands

ISBN-13 (pbk): 978-1-4842-3518-8   ISBN-13 (electronic): 978-1-4842-3519-5
https://doi.org/10.1007/978-1-4842-3519-5

Library of Congress Control Number: 2018935910

Managing Director, Apress Media LLC: Welmoed Spahr
Acquisitions Editor: Jonathan Gennick
Development Editor: Laura Berendson
Coordinating Editor: Jill Balzano

Cover designed by eStudioCalamar.

Cover image designed by Freepik (www.freepik.com)

Distributed to the book trade worldwide by Springer Science+Business Media New York, 233 Spring Street, 6th Floor, New York, NY 10013. Phone 1-800-SPRINGER, fax (201) 348-4505, e-mail orders-ny@springer-sbm.com, or visit www.springeronline.com. Apress Media, LLC is a California LLC and the sole member (owner) is Springer Science + Business Media Finance Inc (SSBM Finance Inc). SSBM Finance Inc is a **Delaware** corporation.

For information on translations, please email rights@apress.com, or visit http://www.apress.com/rights-permissions.

Apress titles may be purchased in bulk for academic, corporate, or promotional use. eBook versions and licenses are also available for most titles. For more information, reference our Print and eBook Bulk Sales web page at http://www.apress.com/bulk-sales.

Any source code or other supplementary material referenced by the author in this book is available to readers on GitHub via the book's product page, located at www.apress.com/9781484235188. For more detailed information, please visit http://www.apress.com/source-code.

I would like to dedicate this book to my lovely wife, Andrea, who was so supportive during the writing of this book.

A special dedication is also extended to my late uncle, Hendrik van As, who helped me kickstart my career in software development.

Table of Contents

Foreword

The .NET community has been re-energized by the enthusiasm building behind open source .NET Core. Engineers who have invested years in .NET and ASP.NET are now able to run their code cross-platform on Windows, Linux, Mac, and more. They can make micro-services and run them in containers as well as within container orchestrators like Kubernetes.

There's a ton of new standards and new architectures to learn and explore. There's new open source libraries and new best practices. REST has cemented itself as a must-know architectural style. We need to learn the principles of REST and how those principles map to features in ASP.NET Core 2.0. We also need to expand our web APIs with the power of GraphQL, which will allow us to query our APIs with this exciting emerging standard. And we need to document our APIs with the Open API specification (Swagger).

The book you're holding now is a fantastic entry point for developers both new and old. You'll learn all about .NET Core from the CLI (command-line interface) on up, then build ASP.NET RESTful web services to power any system's back-end. You'll explore best practices for unit and integration testing your services, then for lock-down services with authentication and authorization using open standards. This book is full of practical examples of how to design modern APIs to power websites and mobile apps.

Finally, you'll examine not only how to deploy your code to on-premises servers or the cloud, but also how to do it with continuous integration and continuous deployment. Check in your services and see them tested and deployed automatically! Your .NET web services are now cross-platform, fast, and modular!

I'm thrilled to have played a small part in the open sourcing of .NET and ASP.NET. I'm looking forward to seeing what you build with the ASP.NET Core 2 open source web framework!

Scott Hanselman

@shanselman

Principal Program Manager, Open Source .NET and ASP.NET

About the Author

Fanie Reynders is a software engineer with over a decade of experience in the software industry, specifically focusing on web and cloud solutions. He is a Microsoft Certified Professional and a Microsoft MVP. Fanie is secretly a cloud technology evangelist obsessed with code, architecture, and shiny new tech. He shares knowledge wherever to whoever will listen. He likes teaching, writing, and vlogging about the things that make him happy. He is the coolest dad. He is originally from South Africa and lives in the Netherlands. Visit his blog at https://reynders.co or follow him on Twitter at @FanieReynders.

About the Technical Reviewer

Gerald Versluis is a full-stack software developer and Microsoft MVP from the Netherlands. He has many years of experience working with .NET technologies, Azure, and Xamarin. Gerald has filled a variety of roles across numerous projects. A great number of these projects involved developing Xamarin apps. Not only does Gerald like to code, but he also is keen on spreading his knowledge and gaining some in the bargain. Gerald speaks, records vlogs, provides training sessions, and writes blogs and articles in his spare time.

Acknowledgments

Writing a book is hard work and takes a substantial amount of time, not only for the author, but also for the other people involved behind the scenes.

First, and foremost, I would like to thank my wife, Andrea, for being by my side every step of the way, supporting me in everything I do. Without her, this book wouldn't have been possible.

I am truly grateful to be part of this literature and would like to extend a special thank you to the staff of Apress, particularly Jonathan Gennick, Jill Balzano, and Laura Berendson, for their time and commitment in helping me to get this book off the ground and published.

To my awesome reviewer and friend, Gerald Versluis, thank you for setting time aside to peer review my work and for providing valuable feedback.

Lastly, but certainly not the least, I want to thank Scott Hanselman for taking time out of his busy schedule to write the foreword. I don't think there is anyone else other than Scott who would be more fitting for the part.

To all my family and friends who supported me during this journey, I would like to extend my gratitude for helping me make this book a reality. If there is anyone who I accidentally left out, this was completely unintentional, but I want to thank you regardless.

Introduction

Do you have interest in designing elegant enterprise-grade APIs that can scale and run on any platform? Are you always looking for the next big thing by staying on the forefront of the latest technologies? Do you want to expand your knowledge by learning ASP.NET Core?

Modern API Design with ASP.NET Core 2 is formulated to help the all-around developer gain useful skills for developing APIs in ASP.NET Core 2 and is based on proven industry patterns and practices, like REST. The book covers a wide range of topics with regards to building as well as deploying scalable and cross-platform API solutions.

In the first chapter, I will introduce you to APIs and the vital role they play in our world today. I will also demystify what REST is and what it means for an application to be RESTful by covering the six principles of REST that were introduced by Roy Fielding.

The second chapter is all about getting familiar with ASP.NET Core by learning what it is and how its features align with REST. You also will look at the different tooling that is available for building an API.

In Chapter 3, you will start to create your first API with ASP.NET Core and learn about the essential aspects of its components, like dependency injection and the application startup bootstrapper.

In Chapter 4, you will delve into the extensibility architecture of ASP.NET Core and learn how to create a custom HTTP server by using the file system to process incoming requests. You will discover the concepts of middleware and routing to process and route requests to the particular receiving logic of your application, as well as how hosted services can help run background tasks.

After a quick introduction of MVC in Chapter 5, you will explore what ASP.NET Core MVC is and how it compares to its predecessor in the previous versions of ASP.NET, and you will learn about implementing an API using ASP.NET Core MVC. I will also cover essential features of the framework, like model binding and model validation, filters, formatters, and application parts.

Chapter 6 is all about configuration as you learn about the new configuration model of ASP.NET Core and the different ways of managing configuration data, which originates from multiple sources, within your application.

I will briefly cover application logging and exception handling in Chapter 7, and you'll learn the different techniques that we can apply to gain useful insights from the application at any given moment in time.

As I move onto the topic of security, you'll learn about the differences between authentication and authorization as well as the different authentication schemes that are available when working with server applications. In Chapter 8, I've also implemented JWT authentication, and you'll learn about protecting sensitive data using the ASP.NET Core data-protection stack, enforcing SSL, and implementing rate-limiting to prevent DoS and DDoS attacks.

Chapter 9 is all about adding extra value to our APIs, as you discover how to implement HATEOAS in an ASP.NET Core application, before moving onto the topic of versioning. Furthermore, you will learn technologies like Swagger and GraphQL to make APIs stand out from the rest.

You'll learn about the importance of testing in Chapter 10, and you'll witness some examples of unit and integration tests before learning how to debug the compiled source code of ASP.NET Core using Source Link.

Marking the end of the book, Chapter 11 is all about hosting and deploying ASP. NET Core applications to different hosts, like IIS, Linux, Docker, and Azure, as well as implementing continuous integration and continuous deployment using VSTS and Azure.

As a final thought, I hope that you enjoy reading this book as much as I enjoyed writing it, and I am very grateful for having such an opportunity to publish my work and experiences.

Using This Book

This book is broken down into different chapters, each covering a range of sections relating to that topic of the chapter.

When a code is discussed, the irrelevant parts of the code might be omitted inside the code block with an *ellipse* (...), for simplicity and to keep the focus on the right place.

Because the technology mentioned in this book is cross-platform, when shell commands are executed, each line will be prefixed with a dollar sign ($) to indicate a new command line and is not indented to be part of the command.

Useful Links

The following are links you may find useful:

- Microsoft .NET – `https://www.microsoft.com/net`

- ASP.NET Core Documentation – `https://docs.microsoft.com/en-us/aspnet/core`

- Visual Studio – `https://www.visualstudio.com`

- Microsoft Azure – `https://azure.microsoft.com`

CHAPTER 1

API Design Demystified

The times have changed—we commute with Uber, overnight with Airbnb, pay with cryptocurrencies, and have breaking news at our fingertips via social media. We snap, chat, and share our lives in real-time—and these kinds of apps make it happen.

What drives most of these apps, however, are *Application Programming Interfaces* (APIs), which are the glue of the connected world we live in. APIs are everywhere, from the doorbell in our smart homes to the traffic updates in our connected cars.

In web development, an API is a set of rules or contracts that dictate how consumers should interact with services by explicitly defining expected inputs and outputs. This is an architectural approach to abstract away the definition from the implementation.

Note   Although other uses of APIs include libraries, frameworks, and operating systems, the scope of this book will focus on the context of web-based APIs.

In this chapter, we will address the importance of APIs by understanding what they are as well as by getting introduced to the different architectural styles of web API design. We will then zoom into the REST architectural style and, by applying the six principles of REST, learn what it means to have a RESTful service.

The Importance of APIs

In today's modern, connected world, the API is one of the most critical elements of cloud-based services. Having billions of services out there for consumption requires good abstraction to promote compatibility, usability, and maintainability.

The API plays a crucial part in the integration of two systems, as it enforces a standardized communication link between them. For example, an electrical drill needs power from an electricity source for it to work. To be able to connect electrical equipment to power sources, we need a wall socket and a plug.

1

© Fanie Reynders 2018
F. Reynders, *Modern API Design with ASP.NET Core 2*, https://doi.org/10.1007/978-1-4842-3519-5_1

In this analogy, the wall socket is the API for providing electricity, and the drill is the consumer, as it uses a specific plug to be able to connect to power. One could, of course, connect the drilling machine directly to the wiring circuit, but it would require more manual work and be very unsafe. Imagine having to hardwire everything in your home; the result would be a mess. The point here is that having a plug and wall-socket mechanism drastically improves interoperability, allowing devices to be pluggable given a standard interface.

Web APIs are no different, as they ensure that systems can communicate seamlessly without the complexity of hardwiring. In fact, an API promotes accessibility by allowing multiple systems to use one implementation of business logic, regardless of their technology stack.

Imagine if the National Weather Service had to explicitly implement a system-integration point for each of its consumer systems. Updates and maintenance would be a nightmare, and that apparently wouldn't scale very well. Instead, implement an API to facilitate the flow of data in one standard way. Doing this also opens up the door to other possibilities, like integration with third-party systems, which can lead to opportunities to monetize on some of the internal components.

Other benefits of providing an API are control and analytics. It is vital that you secure sensitive endpoints, and having a mechanism to control access is paramount. There is a Dutch saying, *"meten is weten,"* which means *measuring is knowing*. Understanding *how* services are used provides useful insights on feasibility and potential optimizations.

APIs can be implemented in many different architectural styles. The most common styles that are used in the industry are RPC, WSDL, SOAP, and REST. When designing an API, it is important to use the right style for the problem at hand, as each of the styles has its advantages and disadvantages.

Note   To keep things in perspective, we will mainly focus on the REST-based architectural style. The others are only mentioned to broaden the understanding within the context of REST.

REST: The Good, Bad, and Ugly

REST is an acronym for *Representational State Transfer,* which is a style of architecture based on a set of predefined principles that describe how networked resources are defined and addressed. A service that implements the principles of REST is called a *RESTful* service.

It is common for web services to have clean, readable, and extensionless *unique resource identifiers* (URIs) or to return data in *JavaScript Object Notation* (JSON) format, but having extensionless URIs and endpoints that return vanilla JSON does not necessarily make the service a RESTful service.

Figure 1-1 shows a typical output of a web service given a certain request and includes a dialog response from a developer who doesn't completely comprehend what a RESTful service is.

Figure 1-1. *Example of a common assumption made by web-service developers*

Let's take a look at a typical scenario involving a web service for managing a user profile. Here are some example endpoints for doing basic *create, read, update, and delete* (CRUD) operations on a profile, returning the results in *Extensible Markup Language* (XML) format:

```
/getAllProfiles
/getProfile?id=2
/createProfile
/deleteProfile?id=4
/updateProfile?name=eddy
```

These endpoints don't look too harmful. The first two endpoints, /getAllProfiles and /getProfile?id=2, get all profiles and get a specific profile with an ID of 2, respectively. The /createProfile endpoint is responsible for creating a new profile, and as you might have guessed by now, the last two endpoints, /deleteProfile?id=4 and / updateProfile?name=eddy, delete and update a specific profile accordingly.

After some time in production, the business requested that more features be added, like the ability to retrieve additional friend information with a specific profile response as well as the capability to search for profiles by name. Typically, developers tend to just implement these capabilities in a *quick and dirty* fashion by adding two more endpoints to the collection, resulting in Version 2 of the service looking like the following:

```
/getAllProfiles
/getProfile?id=2
/getProfileWithFriends?id=2
/searchProfileByName?name=frank
/createProfile
/deleteProfile?id=4
/updateProfile?name=eddy
```

The additional endpoints may meet the requested business requirements but start to make the code very redundant by having the same type of information be served with slightly different aspects of it.

For Version 3 of the service, it is further requested that it support JSON responses on some of the current functionality in order for it to be "RESTful." Keeping to the consistency of naming conventions and to prevent breaking changes (which can be a good thing), the developers might simply add more endpoints to the collection:

```
/getAllProfiles
/getAllProfilesJson
/getProfile?id=2
/getProfileJson?id=2
/getProfileWithFriends?id=2
/getProfileWithFriendsJson?id=2
/searchProfileByName?name=frank
/searchProfileByNameJson?name=frank
```

```
/createProfile
/deleteProfile?id=4
/updateProfile?name=eddy
```

As you can see, by just adding support for an additional output format, you can basically multiply the read operations. Going forward with this pattern would be a recipe for disaster, and one can imagine what the impact would be, given another simple request by the business.

Tip   Unlike apps, the general end users of our applications are not typical business or consumer users, but rather developers of applications. It is crucial that you provide an excellent developer experience when designing APIs.

In the previous example scenario, the web services tended to lean more toward a *remote procedure call* (RPC)–style web service rather than a RESTful service. Having an RPC-style web service is not wrong, but it is important to not confuse the characteristics of REST and RPC.

In an RPC world, endpoints are mere *functions* that get triggered remotely, whereas in a RESTful world endpoints are entities, also known as *resources*.

Properly *designing an API is hard* because requirements tend to change and we need to adapt to the business needs of the day. Implementing patterns like REST will improve the experience of our web services by making them less redundant, more scalable, and more maintainable.

Principles of REST

Originally introduced by Roy Fielding in early 2000, the term *REST* was used to complement the design of HTTP 1.1 and URIs as the architectural style for distributed hypermedia-driven systems.

Some of the most important concerns that a RESTful architecture affects include performance, scalability, simplicity, interoperability, communication visibility, component portability, and reliability. These properties are encapsulated by six principles, which are defined by Fielding as the constraints guiding a RESTful system design.

The **Client-Server** constraint enforces the proper separation of concerns between the UI/consumer and the back-end, which mostly contains the business-logic and data-storage implementations. We can observe this constraint in typical network-based systems like websites. In this style, the client initiates requests to the server, which reacts with triggering responses. Enforcing separation between the client and the server promotes the ability to have them evolve entirely independently from each other given that the interface between them doesn't change.

Often combined with the Client-Server constraint, the **Layered System** constraint dictates that layers should be organized hierarchically, restricting the use of a service to the layers directly beneath and above it. Orchestrating components in layers drastically improves reusability, making them more modular.

Building on the Client-Server style is the **Stateless** constraint. Communication between the client and the server needs to be stateless, meaning that a request should contain all the information necessary for the server to understand and to create context. The client is ultimately responsible for managing session state and cannot rely on the server for directly storing any state data. Does this mean that the actual contents of the state need to be transferred back and forth all the time? The short answer is *no*—it is entirely acceptable for the state to be persisted elsewhere and for the client to include an identifier for retrieving it.

The key feature that associates a system with REST is a **Uniform Interface**. This constraint consists of four essential parts, which are resource identification, resource manipulation, self-describing responses, and state management. These architectural elements are implemented directly through URIs, HTTP verbs, media types, and *Hypermedia as the Engine of Application State* (HATEOAS), respectively.

Note   HATEOAS is also part of the Uniform Interface as well as a constraint of the REST stateless application, which allows a client to have no prior knowledge of how to interact with the server beyond a general understanding of the hypermedia provided by the server.

The **Cache** constraint derives from the Stateless constraint and requires that responses coming from the server are *explicitly labeled* as cacheable or non-cacheable, regardless if they are explicitly or implicitly defined. Responses that are cached allow clients to reuse them later when making similar requests, thus improving speed and latency. Caching can be applied to both the client and the server side.

Caution   It is important to not confuse response cache and application/session state, which can be wrongly interpreted as conflicting constraints of REST. The former refers to short-lived transactional messages, and the latter denotes specific persisted context.

The final and optional constraint is **Code on Demand**, which allows a client to access specific resources from the server without knowledge of how to process them. This style is typically implemented by web-based applications that have clients using a client-side scripting language, like JavaScript. Having the ability to add functionality to a deployed client not only promotes extensibility but can also help to offload some server-side tasks onto the client, making it more responsive.

Apply these six constraints to your API services—then and only then will they become truly RESTful.

Wrapping Up

The key takeaways from this chapter are to realize the importance of APIs as well as know how to design them appropriately and understand what it means to have a RESTful API. Throughout this book, we will mainly focus on the most important features of ASP.NET Core to help implement the principles of REST within APIs.

Now that we have a basic understanding of APIs and REST, in the next chapter we will dive right into the technology that can help facilitate building modern, RESTful APIs by introducing ASP.NET Core.

CHAPTER 2

Introduction to ASP.NET Core

Active Server Pages (ASP) was first introduced in 1998 as Microsoft's flagship development framework for building server-side technologies. It was meant to compete with other web frameworks, like PHP, which was very popular at the time. It was initially developed for creating and running dynamic, interactive web applications. Upon requesting an ASP file, the web server executes any code in the file and returns the result it produces to the browser.

Initially only focused on rendering pure websites in *Hypertext Markup Language* (HTML) on the server, ASP (also known as *Classic ASP*) evolved to become *ASP.NET* in 2002 as part of the *.NET framework*—one of the most used frameworks today.

The ASP.NET framework is the successor to Classic ASP and offers a vast variety of application models for building web-based applications fit for almost any scenario. To date, ASP.NET includes **ASP.NET Web Pages** for, like Classic ASP, creating simple page-driven websites; **ASP.NET Web Forms** for making dynamic form-driven web applications; **ASP.NET MVC** for creating more advanced web applications based on the *Model View Controller* (MVC) pattern; and **ASP.NET Web API** specifically for building APIs.

Fast forward to 2016, when a new variety was born called *ASP.NET Core*. It combined the best of ASP.NET Web Pages, -MVC, and -Web API application models into one application framework, which majorly contributed to the One ASP.NET movement, meaning one extensible web framework.

Note At the time of authoring this book, the latest version of ASP.NET Core was version 2.0. The content referred to is focused toward ASP.NET Core and is limited to the most recent known version only.

© Fanie Reynders 2018
F. Reynders, *Modern API Design with ASP.NET Core 2*, https://doi.org/10.1007/978-1-4842-3519-5_2

As the .NET framework evolved, it became more mature and stable, which was a good thing as it was among the premiere frameworks of choice. The downside was that .NET and ASP.NET were both tightly coupled to the release cycles of Visual Studio, which were slow.

The need for quicker releases was urgent and demanded decoupling from Visual Studio, its languages, and its development frameworks. The resulting modularity allows for faster release cycles and quicker feedback loops, enabling technology to adapt at the same pace as business changes.

What Is ASP.NET Core?

To help you fully understand what ASP.NET Core is, you should first take a step back and wrap your head around the underlining development platform, called *.NET Core*.

The .NET Core framework is a brand-new, lightweight, and modular platform developed by Microsoft and the community for building cross-platform applications and services. It implements the *.NET Standard* protocol to target all platforms in order to deliver a unified experience.

Note   The .NET Standard is not to be confused with the .NET framework or .NET Core as it is intended to serve as a specification that compatible frameworks need to implement to target multiple platforms. More information on .NET Standard can be found at `https://blogs.msdn.microsoft.com/dotnet/2016/09/26/introducing-net-standard`.

One of the key features of this framework is that it is extremely fast and has been one of the top-performing frameworks on the *TechEmpower* benchmarks site (`https://www.techempower.com/benchmarks`).

Furthermore, multiple languages are supported by .NET Core, like C#, VB, and F#, including modern programmatic constructs like generics, *language-integrated query* (LINQ), asynchronous programming, and other features one could expect from a modern language.

Built from the ground up, the ASP.NET Core framework is an open source, cross-platform web platform for developing cloud-based server applications. It can run on both the full .NET framework and the .NET Core framework, which is natively cross-platform, meaning applications targeting ASP.NET Core can run *everywhere*.

ASP.NET Core is optimized for applications deployed both to the cloud or on-premises. Modularity is at the heart of its design, making it extremely flexible and extensible. By using the available tooling for ASP.NET Core, you can develop and run your applications on Windows, Linux, and Mac.

.NET Core vs .NET Framework

Although .NET Core and the full .NET framework share many common components, there are fundamental differences between the two, and choosing between them depends on the scenario at hand.

When there is a need for the application to run cross-platform or have an architecture based on microservices, to promote high availability and scalability, or to run side-by-side with different versions of .NET, then using .NET Core will be the right choice.

Use the .NET framework if the application is currently using the full .NET framework and the recommendation suggested extending instead of migrating, or if there are third-party libraries, technologies, or platforms that do not support .NET Core.

Note   The .NET framework is not obsolete and will still be around and supported for a long time. The .NET Core framework is also not intended to be a replacement for the full .NET framework but rather is built to co-exist with it.

Why Use ASP.NET Core?

ASP.NET Core includes a unified use case for building web-based user interfaces and web APIs. Furthermore, it integrates with other modern client-side frameworks, development workflows, and tools.

The framework contains a cloud-ready, environment-based configuration system out of the box that supports application settings provided in many different formats, all in one simple model. One of the unique features of ASP.NET Core is the notion of making *dependency injection* a first-class citizen within the framework.

Unlike the *HttpHandlers* and *HttpModules* featured in the ASP.NET framework, the new HTTP request pipeline has been designed for more straightforward use, making it much more modular and lightweight.

Inherently, ASP.NET Core can be hosted everywhere (because it is built on top of .NET Core), be it *internet information services* (IIS), self-hosted in its own process, or even hosted inside *Docker*.

Regarding deployments, all components of ASP.NET Core comprise of multiple *NuGet* packages, allowing granular features to be autonomously installed.

The .NET Ecosystem

Now that you have a better understanding of .NET Core and ASP.NET Core, it is beneficial to understand how these components fit into the overall .NET ecosystem. Figure 2-1 provides a bird's-eye view of all the essential parts of .NET.

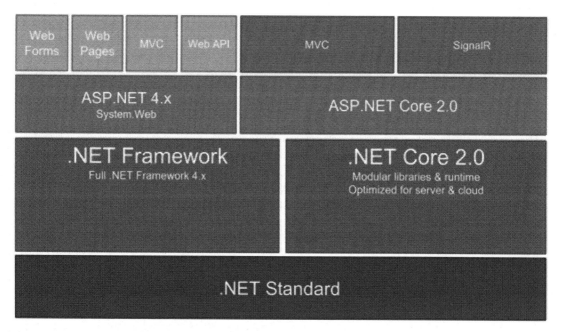

Figure 2-1. *Overview of the .NET platform*

Note   In Figure 2-1, ASP.NET Core hangs over both the .NET framework and .NET Core. This shows that ASP.NET Core and everything built on top of it supports direct compilation for both the .NET framework and the .NET Core framework side-by-side.

ASP.NET Core Features

In the previous section, we briefly covered some of the characteristics of ASP.NET Core. Following this notion, let's now focus on some of the most important features of this framework to highlight how it can relate to implementing a RESTful architecture.

Hosting is a fundamental feature of ASP.NET Core and is at the heart of any server-based application. An application host acts as a container and is responsible for managing the lifetime of the application. The host also contains environment configuration and servers for handling requests. From a REST perspective, hosts and servers satisfy the Client-Server constraint.

The **middleware** feature aligns beautifully with the Layered System constraint from REST. The overall request/response architecture is primarily driven by middleware, which are components that can intercept requests and perform specific logic before possibly invoking the next component in the pipeline or stopping the request entirely.

To have maintainable and extensible code, you need to have loosely coupled components that are easy to test. Using a pattern called **dependency injection** (DI), one can achieve loose-coupling by automatically resolving code dependencies by "injecting" them when needed. In ASP.NET Core, DI is baked right in and available from the start.

One of the unique features of ASP.NET Core is **configuration**, which allows for application settings to be read at runtime from many different sources, like files, from the command line, environment variables, in-memory, encrypted secret stores, or your own tailor-made providers, like an INI file provider.

ASP.NET Core provides an extensive **logging** infrastructure that works with many providers to send entries to many destinations. You can control the level of logging as well as the scope of log entries, which groups log data for similar operations.

As previously mentioned, MVC is an example of an **application framework** supported by ASP.NET Core. Given the nature of the open-ended architectural design, it allows you also to create your own application framework that can run seamlessly on ASP.NET Core.

Tooling Available for ASP.NET Core

Figure 2-2 shows an overview of the tooling available for ASP.NET Core in the Microsoft stack.

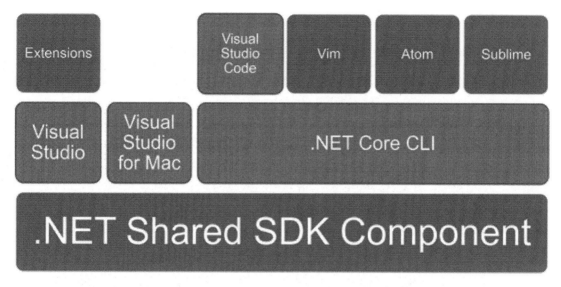

Figure 2-2. Overview of the different tooling available

Starting from the bottom, we have the **.NET Shared Software Development Kit (SDK)** component. This contains libraries with all common APIs for .NET tooling and serves as the foundational layer for all the other tools.

Moving further up, we have the full version of **Visual Studio**, also known as the *Visual Studio IDE*. ASP.NET Core is supported by Visual Studio 2015 (with a minimum of update 3) and upward; however, in this book we'll be making use of the latest version to date, which is Visual Studio 2017.

Visual Studio has the tools you need to quickly create and deploy modern web applications and has support for a wide range of popular languages for web development. Frankly, it has one of the best editors for working with HTML5, CSS3, JavaScript, and JSON. One can seamlessly switch between languages and project types, be it PHP, Java, or Python, LESS or SASS for styling, right through to C# and ASP.NET.

Running software in containerized environments is becoming more and more a thing. Visual Studio 2017 now has built-in support for Docker, a well known container platform, allowing us to run, deploy, and even debug applications running in Docker right within Visual Studio.

When it comes to productivity with modern web frameworks like *Angular* and *Bootstrap*, Visual Studio 2017 is far ahead, providing great *IntelliSense* and advanced language support.

The components that make ASP.NET Core and .NET Core light up within Visual Studio 2017 are all open source, which means you can report an issue if you find a bug, suggest a new feature, or, better yet, submit a pull request yourself.

Out of the box, Visual Studio supports all popular package managers, like NuGet, which offers rich .NET libraries (mostly server side), *NPM* for great tools and utilities, and *Bower* for client-side libraries.

With tools for *Apache Cordova*, you can quickly build cross-platform hybrid web applications using web technologies like HTML5, CSS3, and JavaScript. You might have guessed it: Visual Studio even has support for great emulating experiences with which to run and test our applications.

Visual Studio makes it very easy to work with the cloud by integrating directly with *Microsoft Azure*. You can publish and manage your web applications in the cloud or even remote-debug them directly from within Visual Studio.

Visual Studio allows you to use the source code repository of your choice, be it based on *GIT* or even *TFS* version control. It delivers an excellent experience in managing your source code, gathering bug-tracking and unit-testing statistics, and debugging a wide range of languages like C#, Python, NodeJS, and others.

Quite recently, Microsoft also announced **Visual Studio for Mac**, which is a complete native version of the Visual Studio IDE that runs on Macs to attract more developers who love using their Macs. Version control hosted on any provider is integrated as a first-class citizen, which is great for working seamlessly with other developers on other operating systems. Just like Visual Studio for Windows, Visual Studio for Mac is also packed with the goodness of *Xamarin*, which allows you to create native apps while sharing just one code base for iOS, Android, and Mac OS.

Next on the diagram is the **.NET Core Command Line Interface (CLI)**, which is a new cross-platform toolchain for creating cross-platform .NET applications. It brings most of the tooling features to any terminal interface, be it Command Prompt or PowerShell on Windows or Bash on Linux and Mac.

It can be installed using a native installer, typically on a developer's machine, as well as a shell script, which is used mainly on build servers. The great thing about the .NET Core CLI is that it supports true side-by-side versioning, meaning you can have multiple versions of the SDK installed on one machine.

Built on top of Visual Studio, we have **Extensions**. This extension model allows us to create great add-ons for Visual Studio. There are many recommended extensions available from the *Visual Studio Marketplace* that can help us build awesome web applications using ASP.NET Core, which we will cover during this book.

Furthermore, also quite a new kid on the block is **Visual Studio Code (VS Code)**, which is, in my opinion, one of the best text editors out there for both productivity and development. Developing ASP.NET Core applications within VS Code is a breeze as it leverages the .NET Core CLI beneath the surface for a seamless build and debug experience. It even comes with GIT access baked right in.

As mentioned before, ASP.NET Core runs everywhere; even better, it can be developed in literally any text editor—even Notepad. Some of the other great editors out there are **Vim**, **Atom**, and **Sublime**.

These tools are a prime example of how Microsoft enables productivity so any developer can build great solutions on any platform, for any platform, and it allows developers to use the tools they know and love.

Setting Up the Development Environment

Getting ASP.NET Core is easy. In fact, there are many ways of installing this framework onto your environment. In this section, we will cover two ways of installing ASP.NET Core. Figure 2-3 shows where to get started: `https://www.visualstudio.com`.

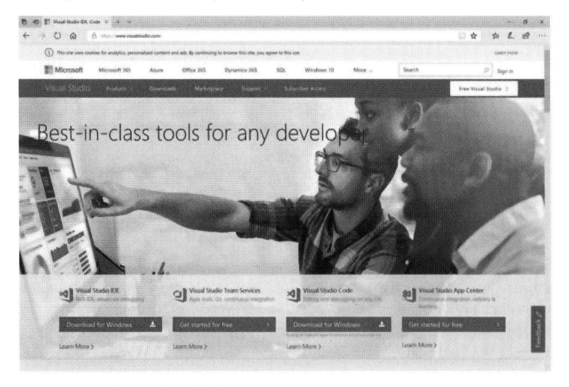

Figure 2-3. *The Visual Studio home page*

The quickest and simplest way to get going is to install the Visual Studio 2017 IDE. This includes a new installer that helps you easily add exactly the modules you want with Visual Studio 2017.

On the Visual Studio home page, hover your cursor over the *Download Visual Studio* button and then click the version you would like to install. The download should only take a quick moment as it is using an online installer to do the heavy lifting.

Tip   Visual Studio 2017 comes in three different editions: *Community*, free for students or individual developers and open source projects; *Professional*, for the professional developer or small teams; and *Enterprise*, for medium to big enterprises. These editions can all run side-by-side, but for this book, the use of the Community edition is just fine.

Figure 2-4 shows the new installer experience as it presents a choice of different workloads to choose from.

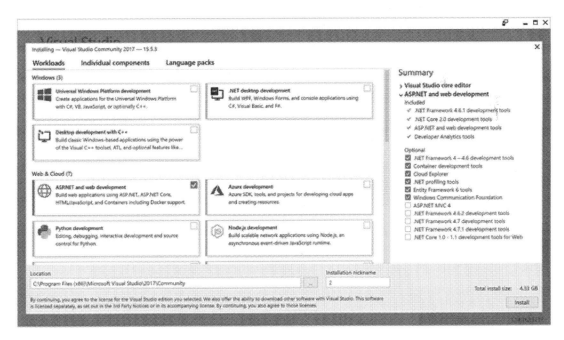

Figure 2-4. *The new Visual Studio 2017 installer experience*

After selecting *ASP.NET and web development workload,* click *Install* and sit back while Visual Studio gets installed with all the goodness of ASP.NET. This workload includes the core Visual Studio editor IDE as well as the ASP.NET Core 2.0 and .NET Core 2.0 development tools.

Note   These instructions assume the installation of the Visual Studio 2017 IDE for a Windows-only environment. To install for Mac, you need to browse to `https://www.visualstudio.com/vs/visual-studio-mac`.

If you instead want to develop with ASP.NET Core 2.0 in Visual Studio Code, you just need to grab the bits separately. Figure 2-5 shows the Visual Studio Code homepage at `https://code.visualstudio.com`, where you can download the latest version of the Visual Studio Code editor for your operating system.

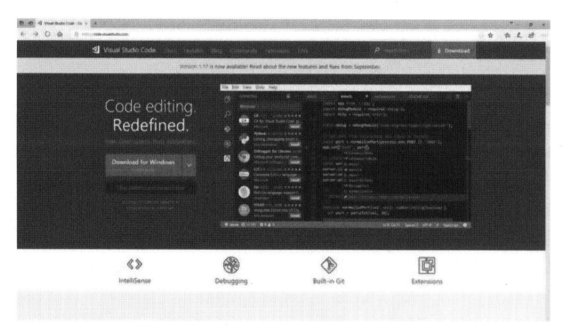

Figure 2-5. *The Visual Studio Code home page*

Now that you have a decent editor, the next thing is to install the *.NET Core SDK*, which includes all the tools you will need for developing cross-platform server applications using ASP.NET Core.

Figure 2-6 shows the download page for the .NET Core SDK at `https://www.microsoft.com/net/core`. Just pick your operating system and follow the installation instructions.

Figure 2-6. *The .NET Core SDK download page*

Note   Both the Visual Studio Code editor and .NET Core SDK will run on Windows, Linux, and Mac.

A Lap Around the .NET Core CLI

Included in the .NET Core SDK is the .NET Core CLI, which is a cross-platform toolchain that acts as a foundation for all other higher-level editors and provides a set of commands for creating, building, testing, running, and deploying .NET applications.

A command is executed by specifying a syntax structure that includes the driver **dotnet** followed by the **command** and its respective **arguments**.

19

Tip   For the sake of simplicity, this section will only cover a limited set of basic and project-modification commands. To get more in-depth information about the .NET Core CLI, use the -h or --help options or browse to https://docs. microsoft.com/en-us/dotnet/core/tools.

The dotnet new command creates a new artifact from a specifically named template. To get a list of installed templates to choose from, use the following syntax:

```
$ dotnet new [-l|--list]
```

Figure 2-7 shows an example output from the console detailing the installed templates.

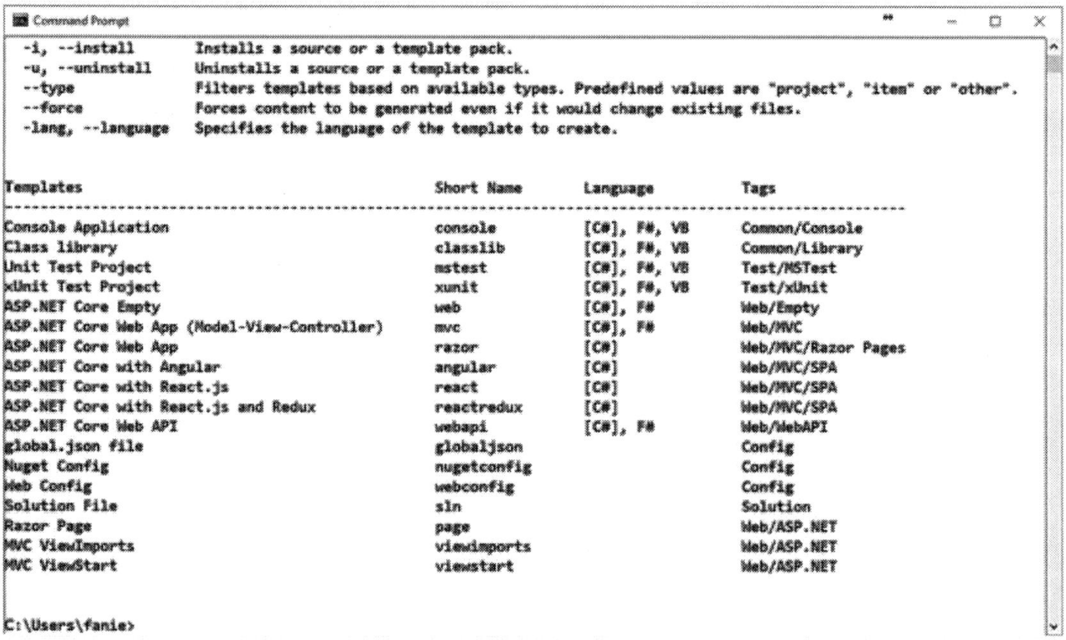

Figure 2-7.   *Output showing installed templates*

The following command syntax creates a new artifact by using the template short name as an argument:

```
$ dotnet new <template short name> [-n|--name]
```

Tip   Although it is optional to specify a name, it is highly recommended. If no name is specified, the name of the current directory will be used instead.

To create a new solution called *AwesomeSauce* and an ASP.NET Core 2.0 Web API project called *AwesomeSauce.Api,* run the following commands:

```
$ dotnet new sln -n AwesomeSauce
$ dotnet new webapi -n AwesomeSauce.Api
```

Tip   Within Command Prompt and Bash you can execute multiple CLI commands one after the other by chaining them using &&.

It is essential that you understand that the preceding commands just created the solution and project artifacts separately. The dotnet sln command is responsible for solution-specific actions. After running the following command to list the projects in the solution, we notice that it does not contain any projects yet:

```
$ dotnet sln list
```

To add the AwesomeSauce.Api project to the AwesomeSauce solution, simply execute the following command (remember to specify the relative path to the project file):

```
$ dotnet sln add AwesomeSauce.Api\AwesomeSauce.Api
```

Rerunning the dotnet sln list command should show the AwesomeSauce.Api project listed as part of the solution.

The dotnet restore, dotnet build, and dotnet run commands are responsible for restoring NuGet packages needed by projects as well as their specific tools, building a project—including its dependencies, and running a project, respectively.

Note   As of .NET Core version 2.0, it is no longer necessary to first run dotnet restore before building and executing. However, it is still a valid command to make use of in continuous-integration scenarios. Prior versions even do require this command to be run before the code is built or run.

Wrapping Up

This chapter was all about getting introduced to ASP.NET Core and wrapping our heads around its features and capabilities as a world-class web framework for building modern APIs. We aligned the features of ASP.NET Core with some of the constraints of REST and explored the different tooling that is available for the ASP.NET Core framework. We learned how to set up our development environment by installing Visual Studio IDE and Visual Studio Code, as well as to understand the basics of the .NET Core CLI tooling for using .NET Core outside of Visual Studio.

In the next chapter, you will create a simple API application using some of the tools previously covered.

CHAPTER 3

Your First API Application

In the previous chapter, we got a concise overview of ASP.NET Core and the relevant technologies. This chapter will focus on helping you create a simple API application using some of the tools we covered previously.

By the end of this chapter, you will be able to create a new API application using one of the pre-defined templates in ASP.NET Core. We will look at how to deal with dependencies across the code base while still maintaining loose coupling between the components. This chapter will also cover the autonomy of the application start-up mechanism to understand how to configure the application initialization process, and, lastly, we will be creating a simple API endpoint that is ready for consumption.

Getting Started

We briefly covered how to create a new web API application using the .NET Core CLI toolchain in the previous chapter. In this section, we will be using the Visual Studio 2017 IDE to do the same thing.

From within Visual Studio 2017, click *File*, then select *New* and click *Project*. If you are a keyboard ninja, you could also do this by pressing *Ctrl+Shift+N*. Figure 3-1 shows the *New Project* dialog that will be displayed.

© Fanie Reynders 2018
F. Reynders, *Modern API Design with ASP.NET Core 2*, https://doi.org/10.1007/978-1-4842-3519-5_3

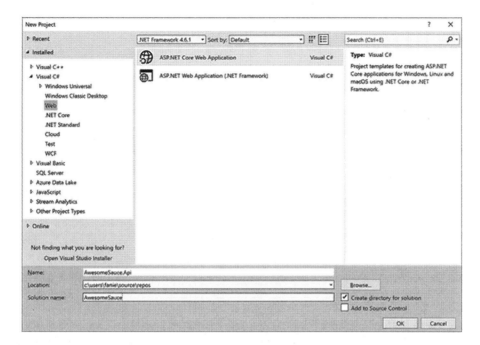

Figure 3-1. *The New Project dialog*

In the *Web* section, we notice two types of ASP.NET web applications, one that is ASP.
NET Core–based and another that is based on the full .NET framework. We need to select
the *ASP.NET Core Web Application* type and give our project a name.

After clicking *OK*, the New ASP.NET Core Web Application template dialog is
presented, which is showcased in Figure 3-2.

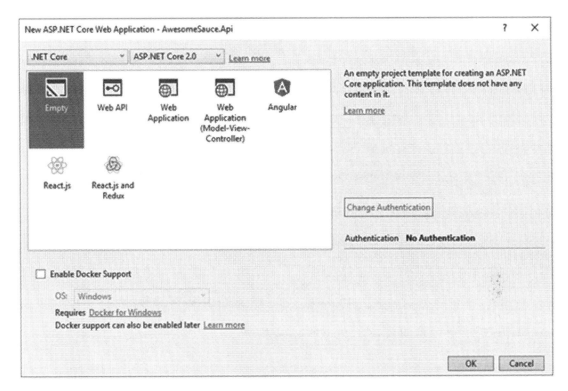

Figure 3-2. *The New ASP.NET Core Web Application template dialog*

Note   At this point, it might be good to mention that the ASP.NET Core project-creation process shares the same template experience in both the Visual Studio 2017 IDE and the .NET Core CLI. You will notice that the templates in Figure 3-2 are the same templates from the output of the `dotnet new -l` command as highlighted by Figure 2-7 in the previous chapter.

In this dialog, we can change the target framework between .NET Core and the full .NET framework as well as switch between ASP.NET Core versions. Let's keep with the defaults, which have the target framework on .NET Core and ASP.NET Core version 2.0.

We are going to start from scratch so we can learn all about the different essential aspects of ASP.NET Core 2.0 applications. Select the *Empty* template and click *OK*.

After the creation of the project, we can explore the structure that was generated from the template, as een in Figure 3-3.

Figure 3-3. *The ASP.NET Core project structure*

An ASP.NET Core project introduces the *Dependencies* node inside the project, which houses all project-level infrastructure dependencies, like Roslyn analyzers, NuGet packages, and SDKs. The Empty template also scaffolded a project with `Program.cs` and `Startup.cs` classes.

One of the great things about .NET Core applications is that we can directly edit the project file from within Visual Studio without having to unload the project first. We can do this by right-clicking on the project and selecting *Edit*.

If you are familiar with any previous versions of ASP.NET, you will immediately notice a striking difference. Compared to the project file of previous versions of ASP.NET, the contents of the project file of ASP.NET Core are now cleaner, with a more straightforward layout. Here are the contents of the `AwesomeSauce.Api.csproj` we just created:

```
<Project Sdk="Microsoft.NET.Sdk.Web">

  <PropertyGroup>
    <TargetFramework>netcoreapp2.0</TargetFramework>
  </PropertyGroup>

  <ItemGroup>
    <Folder Include="wwwroot\" />
  </ItemGroup>
```

```
<ItemGroup>
  <PackageReference Include="Microsoft.AspNetCore.All" Version="2.0.0" />
</ItemGroup>
```

```
</Project>
```

Looking at the `Project` element, there is an `Sdk` attribute that specifies what SDK to use for this project. Specifying the target framework can be done using the `TargetFramework` element, which is .NET Core 2.0 in our example.

Tip   It is also possible to multi-target a project for multiple frameworks by using the `TargetFrameworks` (plural) element.

All files located in the same directory as the project file are included in the project by default. This behavior can be altered by specifying the patterns to include or exclude using the `Folder` element. External dependencies, like other project references, external tools, or NuGet packages, are defined inside an `ItemGroup`. In our example, a NuGet package called `Microsoft.AspNetCore.All` is referenced.

Because we do not need to unload the project to alter the project file, any changes are immediately reflected upon save and can be directly observed in the project structure.

Let's examine the `Program.cs` file:

```
using Microsoft.AspNetCore;
using Microsoft.AspNetCore.Hosting;

public class Program
{
    public static void Main(string[] args)
    {
        BuildWebHost(args).Run();
    }

    public static IWebHost BuildWebHost(string[] args) =>
        WebHost.CreateDefaultBuilder(args)
            .UseStartup<Startup>()
            .Build();
}
```

The starting point of any .NET-based application is a static `Main` function inside a `Program` class. In an ASP.NET Core 2 application, a web host is initiated by calling the `BuildWebHost` function, which invokes `WebHost.CreateDefaultBuilder`, which uses the *Builder pattern* to create a default web host.

Calling the `WebHost.CreateDefaultBuilder` function returns an `IWebHostBuilder` that allows us to pass the application configuration inline or use the provided extension methods to fluently define or override specific configurations, like servers, URLs, logging, web and content roots, and so forth.

The default web host is automatically configured to use the current directory as the content root; load optional configurations from various sources; log console and debug output; use the *Kestrel* server, a new cross-platform web server; and run on IIS if it is available. We will learn more about the configuration model, logging, and servers in coming sections.

Instead of using `WebHost.CreateDefaultBuilder`, we could create a new instance of a `WebHostBuilder` class and then define how we want it to be configured. In the following example, we see the same web host as the default one being created, but instead of hiding all the magic we explicitly define all the configurations that need to be applied to the web host:

```
public static IWebHost BuildWebHost(string[] args) =>
    new WebHostBuilder()
        .UseKestrel()
        .UseContentRoot(Directory.GetCurrentDirectory())
        .ConfigureAppConfiguration(config =>
            config.AddJsonFile("appSettings.json", true)
        )
        .ConfigureLogging(logging=>
            logging
                .AddConsole()
                .AddDebug()
        )
        .UseIISIntegration()
        .UseStartup<Startup>()
        .Build();
```

Dependency Injection

Before we move on, it is essential to understand the concept of *dependency injection* (DI). Having dependencies between the components of an application is inevitable, and if the references to them are not correctly designed, it can have a negative impact on the maintainability of the code. DI is a design pattern to allow instances of objects to be passed to other objects that require them at runtime.

Let's say we have a class called ComponentA that is using ComponentB. The following example shows a typical scenario where no DI is used, and as a result these components are tightly coupled together:

```
public class ComponentA
{
    private readonly ComponentB _componentB;
    public ComponentA()
    {
        this._componentB = new ComponentB();
    }
}
public class ComponentB
{
    public string Name { get; set; }
}
```

Instead of directly referencing an instance of ComponentB, we can decouple it by introducing an IComponent interface to abstract away the implementation and expect an instance of type IComponent in the constructor of ComponentA. In the example that follows, the previous code is now refactored to use DI, having ComponentB implement IComponent so that there is no direct reference to an instance of ComponentB anymore:

```
public interface IComponent
{
    string Name { get; }
}
public class ComponentA
{
    private readonly IComponent _componentB;
```

```
    public ComponentA(IComponent componentB)
    {
        this._componentB = componentB;
    }
}
public class ComponentB: IComponent
{
    public string Name { get; set; } = nameof(ComponentB)
}
```

When we run this code as is, it will result in a `NullReferenceException` error because `ComponentA` is expecting an object of type `IComponent`, and although `ComponentB` implements the `IComponent` interface, there is nothing configured to pass in the required instance of `IComponent` to the constructor of `ComponentA`.

For the code to run without this issue, we need a mechanism to pass the correct instance of a requested type during runtime. This can be achieved by making use of an *Inversion of Control* (IoC) container to register all the required dependencies and their instances. There are many frameworks available on NuGet that provide IoC containers for dependency resolution, namely *Unity*, *Castle Windsor*, *Autofac*, and *Ninject*.

Note   As a general rule of thumb, avoid the explicit instantiation of classes, as doing this results in a tightly coupled system.

ASP.NET Core implements DI as a first-class citizen in its infrastructure and has an IoC container built into its core. Most of the moving parts of this framework are abstracted away from each other to promote extensibility and modularity. This means that if you choose to use your own favorite IoC container instead of the built-in one, you absolutely can.

Application Startup

Now that we understand the concept of configuring and starting a web host, we can focus on the actual bootstrapping configuration of the application. The `UseStartup` method is one of the critical methods that extends an `IWebHostBuilder` and registers a class that is responsible for configuring the application startup process.

The type specified in `UseStartup` needs to match a specific signature to have the host launch the application correctly. The runtime requires the specified startup class to contain two public functions, namely `ConfigureServices`, which is optional, and `Configure`, which is compulsory. For example, let's say that the startup class is defined as `UseStartup<Foo>()`; the structure of `Foo` should match the following:

```
public class Foo
{
    //optional
    public void ConfigureServices(IServiceCollection services)
    {
    }

    //required
    public void Configure()
    {
    }
}
```

Across ASP.NET Core we will notice that dependencies and configurations conform to a certain *Add/Use* style by first defining *what* is required and then *how* it is used. By explicitly specifying components we need, it optimizes performance and thus increases the application's performance, as we only pay for what we use, not the whole thing.

In the `ConfigureServices` method, all the application-level dependencies are registered inside the default IoC container by adding them to an `IServiceCollection`. Expanding on our previous example, we would map a singleton instance of `ComponentB` to an `IComponent` service as follows:

```
public void ConfigureServices(IServiceCollection services)
{
    services.AddSingleton<IComponent, ComponentB>();
}
```

Note   It is also possible to register a dependency that binds to itself instead of using any interfaces by directly expecting the concrete type in the constructor and calling `services.AddSingleton<T>`, where T is the concrete type in this case.

In the startup class, the `Configure` method is responsible for the actual configuration of the application's HTTP request pipeline and is required by the runtime. This method can contain many dependent parameters that are resolved from the IoC container.

Let's build on the previous examples to have our application print out the name of an `IComponent` to the response when invoking it and show the `Configure` method in action:

```
public void Configure(IApplicationBuilder app, IComponent component)
{
    app.Run(async (context) =>
        await context.Response.WriteAsync($"Name is {component.Name}")
    );
}
```

The two variables that are automatically resolved are an `IApplicationBuilder`, which is the mechanism to configure an application's request, and an `IComponent`. The `IApplicationBuilder` extends with a `Run` function, which passes a `RequestDelegate` that writes out the `Name` property of the `IComponent` to the response. Running the application will result in the response being "Name is ComponentB."

It is also possible to configure the application's dependencies and HTTP request pipeline directly inline when defining the web host, without the use of a startup class. Given the default web-host configuration, an inline startup definition could look like the following:

```
WebHost.CreateDefaultBuilder()
    .ConfigureServices(services =>
        services.AddSingleton<IComponent, ComponentB>()
    )
    .Configure(app =>
    {
        var component = app.ApplicationServices.GetRequiredService<ICompone
        nt>();
        app.Run(async (context) =>
            await context.Response.WriteAsync($"Name is {component.Name}")
        );
    })
    .Build();
```

One of the drawbacks of defining the bootstrapping configuration inline is that we can only pass in one parameter as `IApplicationBuilder` to the `Configure` extension method. This forces us to resolve any dependencies by calling `GetRequiredServices` manually.

Note   Configuration sections can be defined inline while creating the web host, inside a separate startup class. When using `UseStartup` for determining bootstrapping configurations in a separate class, it overrides the configuration sections defined inline on the web-host builder.

At times it may be necessary to have different configuration setups for different environments, so ASP.NET Core allows us to explicitly define environment-specific startup configurations by convention. The startup class is defined as `UseStartup(startupAssemblyName: ...)`; the runtime will then look inside the specified assembly for classes called `Startup` and `Startup[Environment]`, with `[Environment]` being the value that matches the `ASPNETCORE_ENVIRONMENT` environment variable. If an environment-specific class is found, it overrides the default one.

For example, if the environment is set as "Development," the runtime will attempt to load `Startup` and `StartupDevelopment`. Inside the startup classes, the same convention applies for the `ConfigureServices` and `Configure` methods as well, whereby the convention is `Configure[Environment]Services` and `Configure[Environment]` respectively.

Creating an Endpoint

Now that we have a good understanding of how ASP.NET Core initializes a web host and bootstraps an application, let's dive right into building a couple of endpoints for consumption.

As explained previously, the `IApplicationBuilder.Run` method ultimately executes when the application runs and accepts a `RequestDelegate` as a parameter, which receives the `HttpContext` object. Referring to the example in the previous section, the response will always be the same, regardless of the URI in the request.

In addition to the `Run` method of `IApplicationBuilder`, there is also the `Use` extension method for intercepting requests that could potentially short-circuit the pipeline or let the request through to the next layer in the pipeline. The `Use` extension method takes in a `RequestDelegate` for providing the `HttpContext`, but also receives a `RequestDelegate` for the next layer.

Note The mention of layers inside the request pipeline refers to the concept of *middleware*. API endpoints are nothing more than middleware being executed in a specific order. We will delve more into the concept of middleware in the next chapter.

In the example that follows, we make use of the Run and Use methods to implement the endpoints /foo and /bar as well as a default fallback for an application:

```
public void Configure(IApplicationBuilder app)
{
    app.Use(async (context, next) =>
    {
        if (context.Request.Path == "/foo")
        {
            await context.Response.WriteAsync($"Welcome to Foo");
        }
        else
        {
            await next();
        }
    });
    app.Use(async (context, next) =>
    {
        if (context.Request.Path == "/bar")
        {
            await context.Response.WriteAsync($"Welcome to Bar");
        }
        else
        {
            await next();
        }
    });
    app.Run(async (context) =>
        await context.Response.WriteAsync($"Welcome to the default")
    );
}
```

The order in which the Run and Use methods define RequestDelegates is significant, as the runtime will execute each layer in precisely the same order as it was created. In the preceding example, the first layer checks the request path of the incoming request. If it matches /foo, it short-circuits the request and directly sends the appropriate response back, else it executes next(), which is the next RequestDelegate layer in the pipeline and so on. If the request manages to bypass all the previous Use layers, it eventually executes Run, which sends the default response back.

Tip   Removing the Run layer from the preceding example will cause the application to only serve requests for /foo and /bar. Any other requests will receive a 404 Not Found response.

Other extensions to IApplicationBuilder are Map and MapWhen, which are more appropriate for working with endpoints. Let's refactor the previous example to make use of the Map and MapWhen methods for implementing the /foo and POST /bar endpoints:

```
public void Configure(IApplicationBuilder app)
{
    app.Map("/foo",
        config =>
            config.Use(async (context, next) =>
                await context.Response.WriteAsync("Welcome to /foo")
            )
        );
    app.MapWhen(
        context =>
            context.Request.Method == "POST" &&
            context.Request.Path == "/bar",
        config =>
            config.Use(async (context, next) =>
                await context.Response.WriteAsync("Welcome to POST /bar")
            )
        );
}
```

The Map and MapWhen methods wrap an IApplication.Use delegate. MapWhen requires an additional predicate in order to apply conditions that stretch further than the request path. In the preceding example, all the /foo requests (regardless of their HTTP method) will invoke the *foo* endpoint, and only POST requests with path /bar will invoke the *bar* endpoint.

This sums up the pure basics of creating simple endpoints in ASP.NET Core. We will learn more advanced routing concepts about endpoints in the next chapter.

Wrapping Up

In this chapter, we covered quite a lot about creating your first application in ASP.NET Core. After exploring the new template experience offered by Visual Studio 2017, we dove right into the inner workings of the new project system and how a web host is created. Furthermore, we got a brief overview of dependency injection and learned the importance and benefits of applying Inversion of Control within our application. We also dissected the application-startup process to completely understand how it works under the hood, and lastly we learned how to implement different API endpoints using some of the provided extension methods on the application builder.

In the next chapter, we will go deeper in the rabbit hole to explore even more exciting concepts of ASP.NET Core's extensibility architecture.

CHAPTER 4

Extensibility Architecture

Extensibility is one of the critical features of ASP.NET Core as it allows for a pluggable system architecture. We could, of course, go into all the extensibility points of ASP.NET Core, but to keep to the scope of APIs, in this chapter we will focus on a specific subset.

This chapter will explain some of the essential aspects of ASP.NET Core from an extensibility point of view. We will learn more about hosts and servers, as well as about creating a custom server. We will revisit the concept of middleware, delving deeper into more advanced scenarios. As mentioned before, RESTful APIs deliver resources located on a specific URI, which can be driven by routing. We will also learn more about routing from a practical standpoint. In the last section of this chapter, we will cover hosted services, which are used for running concurrent background tasks within an ASP.NET Core application.

Hosts and Servers

The concepts of hosts and servers play a vital part in the RESTful architecture. We can implement a host with a server that listens for remote requests by clients in ASP. NET Core, and it will beautifully align with the Client-Server constraint dictated by the principles of REST.

We briefly touched on the web host in the previous chapter. In ASP.NET Core, a host is responsible for the bootstrapping, initialization, and lifetime management of applications. For a web application to run, it requires a host with at least one server for serving requests and responses.

Part of the bootstrapping responsibility is setting the proper configuration for the application. The `IWebHostBuilder` provides built-in functionality to configure the application configuration model and the application services as well as a mechanism to *set* and *get* settings that are key/value based.

© Fanie Reynders 2018
F. Reynders, *Modern API Design with ASP.NET Core 2*, https://doi.org/10.1007/978-1-4842-3519-5_4

We can read and write application settings inline by using the `GetSetting` and `UseSetting` functions, respectively. When calling `UseSetting`, it is important to remember that the provided value will be persisted as a *string* value.

Furthermore, there are also other methods extending `IWebHostBuilder` to configure the host. When something goes wrong during the startup of the application, the default behavior will result in the host's exiting (unless it is hosted behind IIS). We can control this behavior by calling `CaptureStartupErrors` and passing either *true* or *false*, depending on if we want to continue attempting to start the server in the event of an exception.

The `UseContentRoot` setting is defined for specifying the base path of where the host should look for content; without this setting, the host will fail to start. The `UseWebRoot` setting determines a relative path for serving static assets and is based on the path set by `UseContentRoot`.

Applications run on multiple environments, each with a possibly different configuration. ASP.NET Core supports specifying a named environment to run in. The framework includes *Development*, *Staging*, and *Development* as built-in environment names, but we could specify any name for our environment. By default, it reads whatever environment name is configured on the `ASPNETCORE_ENVIRONMENT` environmental variable. We can also explicitly define the environment right on `IWebHostBuilder` by using the `UseEnvironment` method.

Although we covered the mechanism of reading the startup from an external class in the previous chapter, it might be good to add that we can also load the application bootstrapping from multiple external assemblies. Using the `WebHostDefaults.HostingStartupAssembliesKey` key in the `UseSetting` method and then specifying a string value with assembly names separated by a semicolon will scan the specified assemblies for a class named `Startup`.

Servers listen to requests made to specific URLs. On the configuration of the web host, we can specify the URLs where the servers should listen for requests. For this, we use the `UseUrls` function, passing the URLs separated by semicolons. It is important to know that some servers, like Kestrel, also provide a configuration for specifying listening locations. We could, of course, use the server's configuration in conjunction with those specified on the web host, but it's also possible to explicitly prefer the host's URLs to the server's by using the `PreferHostingUrls` method.

In the default template we explored previously you might have noticed that `Run` is called on `IwebHost`; this will run the host, blocking any further execution of the application until the host terminates. We can run the web host in a non-blocking fashion by calling `Start` instead.

Let's conclude with two important interfaces used in hosting: the IHostingEnvironment interface provides context for the current execution environment, like application and environment name as well as file providers for serving content from the web and content roots, while the IApplicationLifetime interface allows for handling events when the application is started and stopped, as well as for providing a method for stopping the application explicitly.

In ASP.NET Core, servers are responsible for reacting to requests made by clients by passing these requests to the application as HttpContexts. By default, ASP.NET Core 2.0 includes two built-in servers: **Kestrel**, a cross-platform HTTP server based on *Libuv*, and **HTTP.sys**, a Windows-only server based on the *HTTP.sys kernel driver*. Figure 4-1 shows a diagram of how servers pass requests to the application.

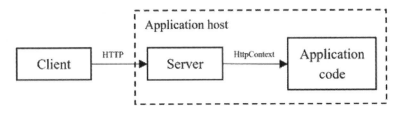

Figure 4-1. *The request map from the client to the application code*

Tip   Although this book only focuses on some aspects of Kestrel, HTTP.sys is not covered in further detail.

Kestrel can be hosted by itself as a standalone process, or inside IIS. It is generally a good idea to use *reverse proxy servers* such as *IIS* or *Nginx*. These act as a gateway when building API or microservices, providing an additional defense layer as they limit the exposed surface area of or integrate better with existing infrastructure.

When using a reverse proxy, the requests are first handled by the reverse proxy server (which is separate from the application) and are then delegated down to Kestrel. Figure 4-2 shows the request interaction when a reverse proxy server like IIS is used.

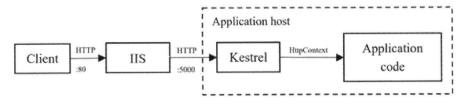

Figure 4-2. *HTTP request interaction with IIS as reverse proxy*

To tell the web host to work behind IIS, we use the UseIISIntegration extension method from IwebHostBuilder. We will configure the host to listen for requests coming from the *ASP.NET Core IIS Module* (ANCM), an IIS module explicitly built for serving requests from IIS to ASP.NET Core.

Note   ANCM must be installed in IIS on the server (or IIS Express on your development machine) for the IIS integration to work. Visual Studio automatically installs ANCM for us on IIS Express. ANCM for servers can be downloaded from `https://aka.ms/dotnetcore.2.0.0-windowshosting.`

As mentioned before, ASP.NET Core is super pluggable. If you want to use another server, you most definitely can. We learned earlier that calling WebHost. CreateDefaultBuilder will automatically configure Kestrel as the server, but we can override this behavior so it uses HTTP.sys instead by using the UseHttpSys extension method. Let's look at the source code of this method to understand what this does beneath the surface:

```
public static IWebHostBuilder UseHttpSys(this IWebHostBuilder hostBuilder)
{
    return hostBuilder.ConfigureServices(services => {
        services.AddSingleton<IServer, MessagePump>();
        // ...
    });
}
```

See something familiar? This method registers a singleton of an IServer as a MessagePump, which is an implementation of HTTP.sys. If you dig deeper, you will notice that MessagePump implements the IServer interface. There is also a UseKestrel method that binds IServer to KestrelHttpServer. Here's the source code for the UseKestrel method:

```
public static IWebHostBuilder UseKestrel(this IWebHostBuilder hostBuilder)
{
    return hostBuilder.ConfigureServices(services => {
        // ...
        services.AddSingleton<IServer, KestrelServer>();
```

```
    // ...
  });
}
```

Note   Order matters when registering dependencies. If we call
`AddSingleton<TInterface, TService>()` multiple times with the same
`TInterface`, the last `TService` registered will override the previous.

Kestrel and HTTP.sys are built-in, but what if we want to use a third-party server,
like FooServer? Another extension on IWebHostBuilder is UseServer, which accepts an
instance of type IServer. Investigating the source of this method will reveal that, again, it
simply registers a singleton of type IServer:

```
public static IWebHostBuilder UseServer(this IWebHostBuilder hostBuilder,
IServer server)
{
// ...

    return hostBuilder.ConfigureServices(services => {
        services.AddSingleton(server);
    });
}
```

Creating a Custom Server

To create our custom server, we simply need to implement IServer, which has the
following signature:

```
public interface IServer : IDisposable
{
    IFeatureCollection Features { get; }
    Task StartAsync<TContext>(IHttpApplication<TContext> application,
    CancellationToken cancellationToken);
    Task StopAsync(CancellationToken cancellationToken);
}
```

Note   ISever requires a set of features to be implemented. You are free to implement just the features needed by your application, but at a minimum it needs to support IHttpRequestFeature and IHttpResponseFeature.

The server we will build is called *AwesomeServer,* an HTTP server that receives specific requests via files that are dropped in a folder on disk (instead of a network port) and then forwards them as proper HTTP requests to the rest of the request pipeline of the application. After the application processes the request, the returning response will overwrite the same file. Figure 4-3 shows a diagram of how a request is read from a file and the returning response is written back.

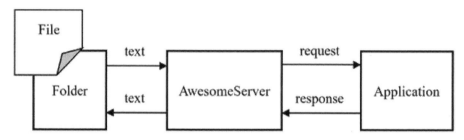

Figure 4-3.   *The high-level architecture of AwesomeServer*

Let's look under the hood of the AwesomeServer class:

```
public class AwesomeServer : IServer
{
    public AwesomeServer(IOptions<AwesomeServerOptions> options)
    {
        Features.Set<IHttpRequestFeature>(new HttpRequestFeature());
        Features.Set<IHttpResponseFeature>(new HttpResponseFeature());

        var serverAddressesFeature = new ServerAddressesFeature();
        serverAddressesFeature.Addresses.Add(options.Value.FolderPath);
        Features.Set<IServerAddressesFeature>(serverAddressesFeature);
    }

    public IFeatureCollection Features { get; } = new FeatureCollection();

    public void Dispose() { }
```

```
public Task StartAsync<TContext>(IHttpApplication<TContext>
application, CancellationToken cancellationToken)
{
    return Task.Run(() =>
    {
        var watcher = new AwesomeFolderWatcher<TContext>(application,
        Features);
        watcher.Watch();
    });
}

public Task StopAsync(CancellationToken cancellationToken)
{
    return Task.FromResult(0);
}
}
```

Starting in the constructor, after adding the two features that are required at a minimum to make `AwesomeServer` an HTTP server, we create a new instance of `IServerAddressesFeature`, adding the folder path from the `IOptions` injected and then adding the feature to the `IFeatureCollection`.

The `IFeatureCollection` contains the capabilities of the server. The `AwesomeServer` has a server listening address and can process requests as well as responses. `StartAsync` and `StopAsync` contain logic for starting and stopping the server.

When `AwesomeServer` starts up, a new instance of `AwesomeFolderWatcher` is created that is responsible for watching a specific folder. To put things in perspective, `AwesomeFolderWatcher` to `AwesomeServer` is the same as *Libuv* is to *Kestrel*.

Here are the contents of `AwesomeFolderWatcher`:

```
public class AwesomeFolderWatcher<TContext>
{
    private readonly FileSystemWatcher watcher;
    private readonly IHttpApplication<TContext> application;
    private readonly IFeatureCollection features;
    public AwesomeFolderWatcher(IHttpApplication<TContext> application,
    IFeatureCollection features)
    {
```

```
    var path = features.Get<IServerAddressesFeature>().Addresses.
    FirstOrDefault();
    this.watcher = new FileSystemWatcher(path);
    this.watcher.EnableRaisingEvents = true;
    this.application = application;
    this.features = features;
}
public void Watch()
{
    watcher.Created += async (sender, e) =>
    {
        var context = (HostingApplication.Context)(object)application.
        CreateContext(features);
        context.HttpContext = new AwesomeHttpContext(features,
        e.FullPath);
        await application.ProcessRequestAsync((TContext)(object)context);
        context.HttpContext.Response.OnCompleted(null, null);
    };

    Task.Run(() => watcher.WaitForChanged(WatcherChangeTypes.All));
    }
}
```

The constructor accepts an IHttpApplication<TContext>, which is an instance of the application, as we as an IFeatureCollection. Furthermore, a new global instance of the standard .NET FileSystemWatcher is created inside the constructor and is configured to watch the folder specified in IServerAddressesFeature.

The Watch method just adds a delegate to the FileSystemWatcher's Created event containing the logic to execute whenever a new file is created in the folder being monitored. Here, we create a new application context, assigning its HttpContext as a new instance of AwesomeHttpContext, which is a specific override of HttpContext created especially for the file system.

After an HttpContext is created that contains an HttpRequest and HttpResponse, we pass it to the application for processing in its request pipeline. When the application finishes the request and returns the response, we signal the completion of the request by calling OnCompleted on the Response property of the HttpContext.

Let's investigate a summarized snippet of AwesomeHttpContext:

```
public class AwesomeHttpContext : HttpContext
{
    public AwesomeHttpContext(IFeatureCollection features, string path)
    {
        this.Features = features;
        this.Request = new FileHttpRequest(this, path);
        this.Response = new FileHttpResponse(this, path);
    }
    public override HttpRequest Request { get; }
    public override HttpResponse Response { get; }
    public override IFeatureCollection Features { get; }

    // ...
}
```

One of the parameters that the constructor of AwesomeHttpContext accepts is a folder path, which is passed to both the Request and the Response properties. FileHttpRequest and FileHttpResponse both inherit from and override the HttpRequest and HttpResponse, respectively.

Now that we have an HttpContext let's quickly take a step back and understand how the request will be translated from plain text in a file. Like the syntax of an HTTP request, the file contents need to match a specific structure. To keep things simple, we will stick to the following format:

{HTTP Verb} {Relative Path}

Now, looking into FileHttpRequest, we see that the file is read, the contents are parsed, and the required parts are built for making a valid HttpRequest that the application can process:

```
public class FileHttpRequest : HttpRequest
{
    public FileHttpRequest(HttpContext httpContext, string path)
    {
        var lines = File.ReadAllText(path).Split('\n');
        var request = lines[0].Split(' ');
        this.Method = request[0];
```

45

```
        this.Path = request[1];
        this.HttpContext = httpContext;
    }
    public override string Method { get; set; }
    public override PathString Path { get; set; }
    public override string Scheme { get; set; } = "file";
    public override HttpContext HttpContext { get; }

    // ...
}
```

When the request passes through the application request pipeline, a response is created and ultimately ends up back on the server. Upon return of the response, we call the OnCompleted method to run specific logic for handling the response. Here is a snippet of FileHttpResponse:

```
public class FileHttpResponse : HttpResponse
{
    public override void OnCompleted(Func<object, Task> callback, object
    state)
    {
        using (var reader = new StreamReader(this.Body))
        {
            this.Body.Position = 0;
            var text = reader.ReadToEnd();
            File.WriteAllText(path, $"{this.StatusCode} - {text}");
            this.Body.Flush();
            this.Body.Dispose();
        }
    }

    // ...
}
```

When calling OnCompleted, we read the response body and write it—together with the status code—to the original file.

Finally, to keep to the *Add/Use* pattern, we create an extension method for wiring up an instance of IServer as AwesomeServer:

```
public static IWebHostBuilder UseAwesomeServer(this IWebHostBuilder
hostBuilder, Action<AwesomeServerOptions> options)
{
    return hostBuilder.ConfigureServices(services =>
    {
        services.Configure(options);
        services.AddSingleton<IServer, AwesomeServer>();
    });
}
```

Now, let's take our custom server for a spin! The application in the following sample is created from the standard *Empty* template, which returns "Hello World" for any request. We add UseAwesomeServer when creating the web host, specifying the folder to monitor:

```
public static IWebHost BuildWebHost(string[] args) =>
    WebHost.CreateDefaultBuilder(args)
        .UseAwesomeServer(o=>o.FolderPath = @"c:\sandbox\in")
        .UseStartup<Startup>()
        .Build();
```

Figure 4-4 shows the console when running the application. Notice that it listens on a folder path instead of a URL.

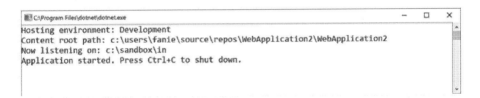

Figure 4-4. *The console output when starting an application with AwesomeServer*

Figure 4-5 shows a sample file that we copy to the c:\sandbox\in directory.

47

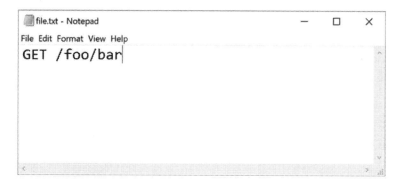

Figure 4-5.   The sample file contents

When dropping the file into the Listen directory, we can see from the logs on the console that the request was successfully processed and the response was then written to the original file. Figure 4-6 shows this in action.

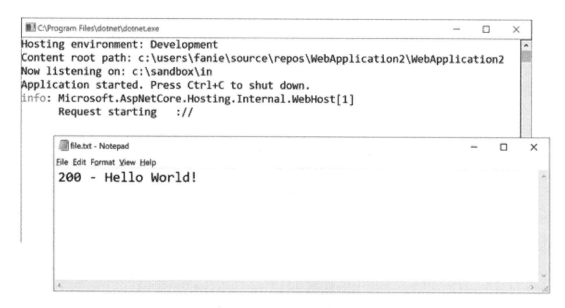

Figure 4-6.   The final result after processing the file

Note   Although using an HTTP server based on the file system isn't particularly useful, the preceding example is used only to show the possibilities for implementing a custom server.

We now have a better understanding of web hosts and servers in ASP.NET Core from an extensibility perspective. In the next section, we'll delve into the request pipeline of an ASP.NET Core application.

Middleware

The components that are assembled within the application request pipeline are called *middleware* and are responsible for handling requests and responses passing through the pipeline. In the context of an HTTP request pipeline, middleware is also commonly referred to as *request delegates*, which are orchestrated using the Run, Map, and Use extension methods.

Each middleware component can perform optional logic before and after it is invoked, as well as choose to pass the request on to the next middleware component in the pipeline. Figure 4-7 demonstrates the flow of a request through the middleware in an application request pipeline.

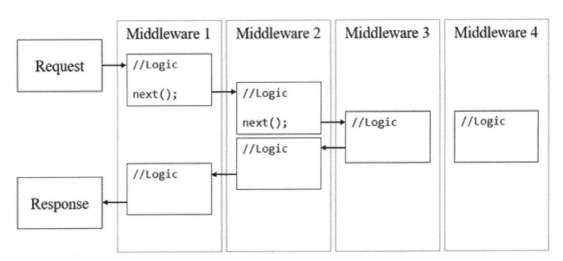

Figure 4-7. *The flow of a request through the middleware components*

In the preceding example, an incoming request passes through the logic of the first three middleware components. At middleware 3, the request is then short-circuited and returns a response, which passes through more logic of middleware 2 and middleware 1. The logic of middleware 4 is not executed in this case.

Having these composable layers of request delegates makes ASP.NET Core extraordinarily extensible, and applications built on ASP.NET Core are almost entirely made out of middleware. This architecture helps ASP.NET Core adhere to the Layered System constraint of REST.

We briefly covered the use of the Run, Map, and Use extension methods in the previous chapter, but let's do a quick refresher to wrap our heads around the construction of middleware. Request delegates can be defined inline (also called inline middleware) or separately in a reusable class.

Here's a configuration application that uses a combination of Run, Map, and Use to invoke middleware inline:

```
public void Configure(IApplicationBuilder app)
{
    app.Map("/skip", (skipApp) => skipApp.Run(async (context) =>
        await context.Response.WriteAsync($"Skip the line!")));

    app.Use(async (context, next) =>
    {
        var value = context.Request.Query["value"].ToString();
        if (int.TryParse(value, out int intValue))
        {
            await context.Response.WriteAsync($"You entered a number:
            {intValue}");
        }
        else
        {
            context.Items["value"] = value;
            await next();
        }
    });

    app.Use(async (context, next) =>
    {
        var value = context.Items["value"].ToString();
        if (int.TryParse(value, out int intValue))
        {
```

```
        await context.Response.WriteAsync($"You entered a number:
        {intValue}");
    }
    else
    {
        await next();
    }
});

app.Use(async (context, next) =>
{
    var value = context.Items["value"].ToString();
    context.Items["value"] = value.ToUpper();
    await next();
});

app.Use(async (context, next) =>
{
    var value = context.Items["value"].ToString();
    context.Items["value"] = Regex.Replace(value, "(?<!^)[AEUI](?!$)",
    "*");
    await next();
});

app.Run(async (context) =>
{
    var value = context.Items["value"].ToString();
    await context.Response.WriteAsync($"You entered a string: {value}");
});
}
```

Let's break it down: app.Use("/skip", ...) branches the pipeline matching the given request URL and then executes the sub-application. When we execute /skip, we see "*Skip the line!*" as the response.

Back on the main branch, the first middleware checks if the value query parameter is a number, then it short-circuits the pipeline; when the value query parameter is a string value, then it assigns a context variable to hold the value and calls next(); to invoke the following request delegate in the pipeline. When we execute /?value=123 we get back "*You entered a number: 123*" as the response.

The second middleware updates the value context variable to an uppercase value and then calls next(); to invoke the third middleware component, which updates the value context variable by replacing all vowels with a "*" character and then calls next(); to invoke the last request delegate.

App.Run(...) ultimately executes after the uppercase and masking middleware have modified the value. If we execute /?value=fanie+reynders we get back "*You entered a string: F*N** R*YND*RS*" as the response.

Note   It is imperative to understand that ordering matters when working with request delegates in the application pipeline. The order in which it is defined is the order in which the components will execute the request and the reverse thereof for the response during runtime.

Let's take the previous example and refactor the *number check* request delegate into a separate class called NumberCheckerMiddleware to make it reusable.

```
public class NumberCheckerMiddleware
{
    private readonly RequestDelegate next;
    public NumberCheckerMiddleware(RequestDelegate next)
    {
        this.next = next;
    }

    public async Task Invoke(HttpContext context)
    {
        var value = context.Request.Query["value"].ToString();
        if (int.TryParse(value, out int intValue))
        {
            await context.Response.WriteAsync($"You entered a number:
            {intValue}");
```

```
        }
        else
        {
            context.Items["value"] = value;
            await next(context);
        }
    }
}
```

Middleware as a separate class is preferred over inline middleware in ASP.NET Core. Writing middleware as classes requires a class with at least one constructor that expects the next RequestDelegate in the pipeline as a parameter and an Invoke method that receives the HttpContext. Regarding the rest of the code changes, it was pretty much copy-and-paste, except when invoking next(...), as it required the HttpContext as a parameter.

Instead of calling the number checker delegate inline, we now use app.UseMiddl eware<NumberCheckerMiddleware>(). We could go a step further and write extension methods for our middleware:

```
public static class NumberCheckerMiddlewareExtensions
{
    public static IApplicationBuilder UseNumberChecker(this
    IApplicationBuilder app)
    {
        return app.UseMiddleware<NumberCheckerMiddleware>();
    }
}
```

This allows us to call app.UseNumberChecker(), which makes things more readable. Here's what the code could look like when applying these practices:

```
public void Configure(IApplicationBuilder app)
{
    app.Map("/skip", (skipApp) => skipApp.UseSkipApp());
    app.UseNumberChecker();
    app.UseUpperValue();
    app.UseVowelMasker();
    app.Run(async (context) =>
```

```
    {
        var value = context.Items["value"].ToString();
        await context.Response.WriteAsync($"You entered a string:
{value}");
    });
}
```

ASP.NET Core comes with many standard middleware options built in for authentication, CORS configuration, response caching and compression, routing, managing sessions, static files, and managing URL rewriting. In the next section, we will look at how the routing middleware can help us when working with URLs in our application.

Routing

Request routing is one of the fundamental features of any API application and helps with identifying resources as *Uniform Resource Identifiers* (URIs). In ASP.NET Core we make use of the RouterMiddleware, which gives us the functionality to map an incoming request to a route handler.

Application routes are configured when the application starts up, and they can optionally extract values from request URLs to be used further along in the pipeline. Because the routes are defined based on a specific template, it is also possible to generate URLs for particular routes during runtime.

An application uses one collection of routes, and when a request comes into the handler, it scans each route in order and matches the given request to the appropriate template.

Note   This section describes the low-level basics of routing and is not detailing any specifics of routing from the MVC framework.

To start using the routing functionality, we follow the *Add/Use* pattern to opt in to the routing feature within ConfigureServices of the application Startup:

```
public void ConfigureServices(IServiceCollection services)
{
    services.AddRouting();
}
```

```
public void Configure(IApplicationBuilder app)
{
    app.UseRouter(...);
}
```

The UseRouter extension method either receives an IRouter or an Action<IRouteBuilder>. For simplicity, we'll use the Action<IRouteBuilder> variant. Using the provided IRouteBuilder, we can wire up all our necessary routes for the application.

```
app.UseRouter(builder=>
{
    builder.MapRoute(string.Empty, context =>
    {
        return context.Response.WriteAsync($"Welcome to the default route!"));
    }

    builder.MapGet("foo/{name}/{surname?}", (request, response, routeData) =>
    {
        return response.WriteAsync($"Welcome to Foo, {routeData.
        Values["name"]} {routeData.Values["surname"]}"));
    }

    builder.MapPost("bar/{number:int}", (request, response, routeData) =>
    {
        return response.WriteAsync($"Welcome to Bar, number is {routeData.
        Values["number"]}"));
    }
});
```

The builder has many extension methods for building routes for specific types of requests, and each one receives a route template and request delegate. When using the RoutingMiddleware, we should always specify a default handler, which is what we do when calling builder.MapRoute(...), specifying an empty route template and passing a request delegate that writes "*Welcome to the default route!*" to the response.

Using builder.MapGet(...) and builder.MapPost(...) will cause the router to catch all the GET and POST requests, respectively, matching the given templates. Route data variables can be specified in the templates using the *curly braces convention* and consumed by using the provided RouteData parameter.

The second route, foo/{name}/{surname?}, will match a URL starting with *"foo/"* followed by a value that will be allocated as name and then an optional value as surname. Optional route variables are denoted using the *question mark* (?), making them nullable.

Routes can also be further constrained by data type, as seen on the third route, where POST requests are matched using bar/{number:int}. The value of the number route variable must be a valid number for the resolver to match the route. There are many route constraints available that we can apply on route templates, ranging from typed or ranges to regular expressions.

Generating a URL for a specific route is quite straightforward. Compile a RouteValueDictionary containing all the route data necessary, create a new VirtualPathContext, and pass in the HttpContext, RouteValueDictionary, and route name. By selecting a specific IRoute from the builder's route collection, we can generate a relative URL by calling GetVirtualPath.

```
builder.MapRoute(string.Empty, context =>
{
    var routeValues = new RouteValueDictionary
    {
        { "number", 456 }
    };

    var vpc = new VirtualPathContext(context, null, routeValues, "bar/
    {number:int}");
    var route = builder.Routes.Single(r => r.ToString().Equals(vpc.
    RouteName));
    var barUrl = route.GetVirtualPath(vpc).VirtualPath;
    return context.Response.WriteAsync($"URL: {barUrl}");
});
```

Tip   To learn more about routing in ASP.NET Core, please refer to the fundamentals section of the ASP.NET Core Documentation at https://docs.microsoft.com/en-us/aspnet/core/fundamentals/routing.

Hosted Services

A hosted service provides a mechanism for running background tasks within the lifetime scope of the application. It is quite handy in scenarios where long-running tasks need to run in the background of an application continuously.

ASP.NET Core provides the `IHostedService` interface for creating hosted services. Let's take a look at its signature.

```
public interface IHostedService
{
    Task StartAsync(CancellationToken cancellationToken);
    Task StopAsync(CancellationToken cancellationToken);
}
```

The `StartAsync` method will fire when the host starts up the hosted service, and `StopAsync` will be executed once the host is shutting down.

Let's put this to the test! A practical example of a hosted service implementation is data synchronization. In this case, we have an external service providing our application with comments data. To prevent too many calls to this external service and to have the risk of being blocked, we can implement a hosted service that downloads the comments locally for our application to consume safely.

Here's a snippet of the implementation class called `AwesomeHostedService`:

```
public class AwesomeHostedService : IHostedService
{
    private readonly IHostingEnvironment env;

    public AwesomeHostedService(IHostingEnvironment env)
    {
        this.env = env;
    }

    public async Task StartAsync(CancellationToken cancellationToken)
    {
        var client = new HttpClient();
        var file = $@"{env.ContentRootPath}\wwwroot\comments.json";
        while (true)
        {
```

57

```
        var response = await client.GetAsync("https://api.external.com/
        comments");
        using (var output = File.OpenWrite(file))
        using (var content = await response.Content.
        ReadAsStreamAsync())
        {
            content.CopyTo(output);
        }
        Thread.Sleep(60000);
    }
}

public Task StopAsync(CancellationToken cancellationToken)
{
    return Task.FromResult(0);
}
}
```

When the hosted service starts up, we use an `HttpClient` to get all the available comments from the external service's API and save them locally to disk as a JSON file. By injecting the `IHostingEnvironment`, we can get the content root path wherein the `wwwroot` folder resides. This job is executed indefinitely every minute.

Now that we have implemented a hosted service, we need to tell the application configuration about it. In the `ConfigureServices` function of the `Startup` class, we register a singleton of `AwesomeHostedService` as `IHostedService`. When the host starts up, it will then load all the instances of `IHostedService` and start them accordingly.

```
public void ConfigureServices(IServiceCollection services)
{
    services.AddSingleton<IHostedService, MyAwesomeHostedService>();
}
```

Wrapping up

What an exciting chapter this was! We learned plenty of great things about web hosts and servers in ASP.NET Core. We also looked a little more in-depth at the concept of middleware and discovered that most of ASP.NET Core's infrastructure is based on request delegates living inside an application request pipeline. We also briefly covered the routing middleware, allowing us to specify individual routes for specific request delegates within our application.

Looking back, it was quite a mouthful of code examples to follow along with and try by yourself. In the next chapter, we'll dive into MVC to learn more about this framework for ASP.NET Core.

CHAPTER 5

MVC

This chapter will focus on the implementation of the MVC pattern within ASP.NET Core, specifically from an API perspective as a fully functional web framework. We will explore how data are mapped from HTTP requests and bound to action parameters and strongly typed models, as well as how these models are validated before any data processing happens.

At the end of this chapter, we will also have a broader understanding of how controllers work and grasp the importance of action methods to handle incoming requests. We will learn all about filters and how they can help by executing code before and after the processing of requests in the pipeline.

Returning the appropriate responses is crucial in APIs, and formatting these responses is essential when dealing with many different types of responses. In this chapter, we will also look at how content negotiation uses formatters to return data in specific formats for specific requests and how we can create custom response formatters for serving particular responses.

The last section will briefly cover *application parts*, a new concept in ASP.NET Core that allows applications to be much more modular than before by discovering MVC components from within the application context or external assemblies.

The MVC Pattern

Model View Controller (MVC) is a software design pattern for implementing web applications with user interfaces, and it is used to separate the concerns of three major components, which are models, views, and controllers. This architectural pattern has been around for many years, and it strives to promote code reuse and simultaneous development.

© Fanie Reynders 2018
F. Reynders, *Modern API Design with ASP.NET Core 2*, https://doi.org/10.1007/978-1-4842-3519-5_5

Controllers are the main entry point and handle requests initiated from user interaction. Logic is performed from within the controller, and then it potentially creates a *model*, which houses the state of the application and the business logic around it. The model is then passed by the controller to a *view*, which has the responsibility of rendering a user interface, possibly containing the data from the model. Figure 5-1 shows the interaction of these three components.

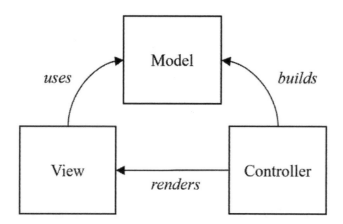

Figure 5-1. *The communication between the parts of the Model View Controller pattern*

MVC in ASP.NET Core

ASP.NET Core MVC is an application framework built on top of ASP.NET Core that allows us to make dynamic web applications with a clean separation of concerns. Compared to its predecessor, ASP.NET MVC (version 1 to 5), the new ASP.NET Core MVC version is open source, lightweight, and redesigned from the ground up to be faster and smaller than before. Its design gives us control entirely over markup and promotes testability within our applications.

When we look at the previous version of ASP.NET, two of the application models it contains are MVC and Web API. The MVC application model was initially intended for rendering views and is used in interactive web applications, whereas Web API was designed to provide data responses, mainly as XML and JSON formats that are used in web APIs.

When we investigate the different components in these application models, we notice that they each contain identical features. Although it may seem like they are sharing these elements among themselves, in reality they are not. Figure 5-2 shows a comparison of the components in MVC 5.x and Web API 2.x in the earlier versions of ASP.NET.

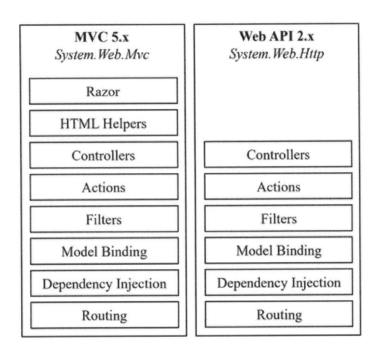

Figure 5-2. *A component comparison between ASP.NET MVC 5.x and ASP.NET Web API 2.x*

The new ASP.NET Core MVC framework unifies the web UI and web API concepts by genuinely sharing the key components that make up web applications. Inherently it is cross-platform due to the infrastructure of .NET Core and benefits from the same hosting mechanism as ASP.NET Core. Furthermore, ASP.NET Core MVC introduces brand-new concepts for working with user interfaces, like *view components*, *razor pages*, and *tag helpers*.

In ASP.NET Core MVC, the controllers, actions, filters, model binding, dependency injection, and routing components are shared in one unified application request pipeline. Think of MVC in ASP.NET Core as a sub-application middleware containing an inner middleware infrastructure.

Naming things is hard. During the development of ASP.NET Core, it was initially called *ASP.NET vNext*, then renamed to *ASP.NET 5* and contained MVC, which was called *MVC 6*. Confusion about compatibility and interoperability started to arise from developers in the community until the team decided to reboot and chose the name ASP.NET Core—one web framework that contains reusable modules, leaving MVC to be just a module referred to as ASP.NET Core MVC.

Note   The contents of this book describing MVC is limited to the scope of APIs only and will not contain the other features that are exclusively used for rendering UIs.

Controllers and Actions

In ASP.NET Core MVC, controllers are used to logically group a section of an application with a set of standard actions or endpoints. They provide the infrastructure for executing action methods. Actions are just functions that can accept parameters, do some logic, and return a specific result, which is then propagated down to the HTTP response at the end.

Action methods can be used to return views for UI-based web applications as well as data in different formats for API-based web applications. From the request pipeline, the routing mechanism relays a request to a specific action method contained inside a controller. Figure 5-3 shows a diagram of the request's journey to the action method.

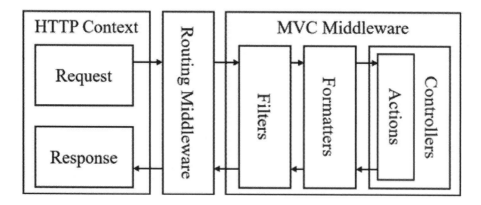

Figure 5-3. *The flow of a request through the pipeline to action methods and back*

Controllers and actions can be defined in many ways inside ASP.NET Core. By default, controller classes reside in the `Controllers` folder in the root of the application and inherit from the `Microsoft.AspNetCore.Mvc.Controller` abstract class. The following example shows how this is done:

```
namespace Awesome.Api.Controllers
{
    public class People : Controller
    {
        // ...
    }
    // or
    public class CustomersController : Controller
    {
        // ...
    }
}
```

Alternatively, controllers can also be defined by using the built-in convention, without the need to inherit from `Microsoft.AspNetCore.Mvc.Controller`, and are also referred to as *Plain Old CLR Object* (POCO) classes. The convention for POCO classes is to have their name suffixed with *"Controller"* as in the following example:

```
namespace Awesome.Api.Controllers
{
    public class PeopleController
    {
        // ...
    }
}
```

Note that in the preceding example the `PeopleController` class does not inherit from the `Controller` base class. It is also possible to completely drop the *"Controller"* suffix on POCO classes by applying the `[Controller]` attribute on the classes that need to be classified as controllers. But what about normal classes that happen to have a *"Controller"* suffix? To prevent these normal POCO classes from being marked as controllers, we can apply the [NonController] attribute on them to negate the convention:

```
namespace Awesome.Api.Controllers
{
    [Controller]
    public class Ships
    {
        // ...
    }
}

namespace Awesome.Api.Models
{
    [NonController]
    public class ShipyardController
    {
        // ...
    }
}
```

If we investigate the source code of ASP.NET Core MVC, we will notice that this is exactly how the base class ControllerBase works. Classes that inherit from Controller, which inherits from ControllerBase, will automatically get the [Controller] attribute because they reside in the ControllerBase class.

When working with an IoC container for injecting dependencies, it is advised to follow the *Explicit Dependency Principle,* which means using the constructor of a class and explicitly defining parameters as receiving dependencies.

```
namespace Awesome.Api.Controllers
{
    public class PeopleController
    {
        private readonly IMyService _myService;
        public PeopleController(IMyService myService)
        {
```

```
        this.myService = myService;
    }
    // ...
}
}
```

Note   The controller abstracts the user interface from the back-end, and as a good practice it is important to also keep business logic out of controllers by delegating the heavy lifting to services instead.

Actions are defined using public methods with potential input parameters, and they can return any type, but mostly the return type is IActionResult. Action methods also can adhere to explicit and implicit conventions by prefixing the method names with one of the HTTP verbs or by using the [HttpGet], [HttpPut], [HttpPost], [HttpDelete], [HttpHead], [HttpOptions], and [HttpPatch] attributes.

Just like in the case of non-controllers, methods that happen to be prefixed with any of the HTTP verbs can be de-classified as action methods by using the [NonAction] attribute.

```
public class PeopleController
{
    public IActionResult Get()
    {
        // ...
    }

    public IActionResult GetOne(int id)
    {
        // ...
    }

    [HttpGet]
    public IActionResult FindPerson(string query)
    {
        // ...
    }
```

```
public IActionResult Post(Person person)
{
    // ...
}

[HttpDelete]
public IActionResult RemovePerson(int id)
{
    // ...
}

[NonAction]
public IActionResult GetCurrentTime(int id)
{
    // ...
}
}
```

Using POCO classes as controllers is great, but we can benefit from more built-in goodness by having controllers inherit from the `Controller` base class. For empty responses, it provides helper methods like `Ok`, `NotFound`, and `BadRequest` to respond with the proper HTTP status codes of 200, 404, and 400, respectively. We can also do redirection by using the `Redirect`, `LocalRedirect`, or `RedirectToRoute` methods. When working with non-empty responses, we can use the formatted response helper methods `Ok`, `Json`, `File`, or `Content` for APIs and `View` for rendering HTML.

When working with content negotiation, it is better to use non–type specific methods like `Ok`, `BadRequest`, `Created`, and so forth. Here is a typical controller containing some of the helper methods mentioned:

```
public class PeopleController : Controller
{
    private readonly IPeopleService _peopleService;

    public PeopleController(IPeopleService peopleService)
    {
        this._peopleService = peopleService;
    }
```

```
    public IActionResult Get()
    {
        var people = _peopleService.GetAllPeople();

        return Ok(people);
    }

    public IActionResult Get(int id)
    {
        if (_peopleService.DoesExists(id))
        {
            var person = _peopleService.GetOnePerson(id);

            return Ok(person);
        }
        return NotFound();
    }

    public IActionResult Post(Person person)
    {
        if (_peopleService.Validated(person))
        {
            _peopleService.Create(person);

            return CreatedAtAction(nameof(this.Get), person.Id);
        }
        return BadRequest();
    }
}
```

If you don't want to use the provided Controller class and like to stick to the POCO style convention, it is possible to achieve the same result by just returning a new instance of an IActionResult. Here's a snippet of the same code but refactored using the POCO style:

```
public class PeopleController
{
    // ...
```

```
    public IActionResult Get()
    {
        var people = _peopleService.GetAllPeople();
        return new OkObjectResult(people);
    }

    public IActionResult Get(int id)
    {
        if (_peopleService.DoesExists(id))
        {
            var person = _peopleService.GetOnePerson(id);
            return new OkObjectResult(person);
        }
        return new NotFoundResult();
    }

    // ...
}
```

Let's now add routing to our endpoints. We covered some of the aspects of routing in Chapter 4, and specifically in the MVC world we can use routing to bind requests coming from certain routes to action methods.

There are two ways of defining routes for an MVC application—namely, using the IRouteBuilder and using attribute-based routing. We've seen some examples of IRouteBuilder previously, but here's a quick example of the Configure method in a Startup in the context of MVC:

```
public void Configure(IApplicationBuilder app, IHostingEnvironment env)
{
    app.UseMvc(builder =>
    {
        builder.MapRoute("default", "api/{controller}/{action}/{id?}"));
    });
}
```

In the preceding example, we create a global route to catch all relevant requests with a URL matching [controller]/[action]/ followed by an optional identification number. From a REST perspective, it is better to infer the action methods by HTTP verbs instead, which is where attribute routing can come in handy.

As the name suggests, attribute routing allows us to explicitly define routes for endpoints directly on controllers and action methods. In the following example, we see a typical controller making use of attribute-based routing:

```
[Route("api/[controller]")]
public class PeopleController
{
    // GET api/people
    [HttpGet("")]
    public IEnumerable<string> Get()
    {
        // ...
    }

    // GET api/people/top
    [HttpGet("top/{n}")]
    public IEnumerable<string> GetTopN(int n)
    {
        // ...
    }

    // POST api/person
    [HttpPost("~/api/person")]
    public IEnumerable<string> Post(Person person)
    {
        // ...
    }
}
```

In my opinion, this is much more declarative than using the IRouteBuilder directly. Using the [Route] attribute on the controllers defines the base route for all the underlying actions, and then each action can contain one or more *relative* route templates specified in the [Http...] attributes, except when they start with a tilde character (~), which will override the base, as seen on the third action method.

Using conventions in our coding makes things a whole lot easier by inferring some of the obvious plumbing. The architecture of ASP.NET Core MVC even allows us to change the conventions if we prefer something more declarative. Let's look at the signature of the IApplicationModelConvention interface provided by the framework to implement custom conventions within MVC:

```
public interface IApplicationModelConvention
{
    void Apply(ApplicationModel application);
}
```

The Apply function receives an ApplicationModel, which is a representation of our MVC application. An ApplicationModel contains a collection of ControllerModel objects, which contains a collection of ActionModel objects. The goal of the convention design is to map whatever class adheres to a specific convention into the abstraction structure provided.

Easy enough? Let's take it for a test drive and implement our own convention that uses the *"Api"* suffix instead of the *"Controller"* suffix for marking POCO classes as controllers. Furthermore, we want our routes to be inferred from the namespace in this example. The implementation would look a little like the following:

```
public class AwesomeApiControllerConvention : IApplicationModelConvention
{
    public void Apply(ApplicationModel application)
    {
        var controllers = Assembly
            .GetExecutingAssembly()
            .GetExportedTypes()
            .Where(t => t.Name.EndsWith("Api"));

        foreach (var controller in controllers)
        {
            var controllerName = controller.Name.Replace("Api", "");

            var model = new ControllerModel(controller.GetTypeInfo(),
            controller.GetCustomAttributes().ToArray());
            model.ControllerName = controllerName;
            model.Selectors.Add(new SelectorModel
            {
```

```
        AttributeRouteModel = new AttributeRouteModel()
        {
            Template = $"{controller.Namespace.Replace(".", "/")}/
            {controllerName}"
        }
    });

    foreach (var action in controller.GetMethods().Where(p =>
    p.ReturnType == typeof(IActionResult)))
    {
        var actionModel = new ActionModel(action, new object[] {
        new HttpGetAttribute() })
        {
            ActionName = action.Name
        };
        actionModel.Selectors.Add(new SelectorModel());
        model.Actions.Add(actionModel);
    }
    application.Controllers.Add(model);
    }
  }
}
```

It all starts by scanning the current assembly for public classes that have a name ending in *"Api"*. For each of these classes, a ControllerModel is created, assigning the controller's name as whatever the name of the class is (excluding *"Api"*) and setting its route template as the namespace with forward slashes.

For each public method that has a return type of IActionResult, a new instance of an ActionModel is created, wiring the appropriate action name in place. Once all the actions have been registered, they are added to their applicable ControllerModel, which is then added to the ApplicationModel.

All that is left to do is tell ASP.NET Core about this convention. We can either replace the default convention or add to it. In the following example, you can see how the custom convention is wired inside the `ConfigureServices` method by adding it to the conventions list:

```
public void ConfigureServices(IServiceCollection services)
{
    services
        .AddSingleton<IPeopleRepository,PeopleRepository>()
        .AddMvc((o) =>
        {
            o.Conventions.Add(new AwesomeApiControllerConvention());
        });
}
```

Using the following POCO class, we can test out the custom convention. Note that it is in a special namespace that declares its route and contains a name that ends with *"Api"*:

```
namespace Api.People
{
    public class NamesApi
    {
        private readonly IPeopleRepository people;
        public NamesApi(IPeopleRepository people)
        {
            this.people = people;
        }
        public IActionResult Get()
        {
            return new OkObjectResult(people.All);
        }
    }
}
```

Now, after a quick build and run, it is time to test out the new convention! Use a browser or any other HTTP client when making the request GET `api/people/names`, and you will notice the expected response returned.

Model Binding and Validation

In ASP.NET Core MVC, incoming requests are mapped to parameters of action methods, which can be simple types like *integers* and *strings* or more complex types like complete *data transfer objects* (DTOs). This process of binding HTTP requests to method parameters is called *model binding* and abstracts away the mapping logic to prevent rewriting the same map over and over.

For example, with the route template `api/{controller}/foo/{action}/{name?}`, the request `GET /api/people/foo/search/fanie?top=5` will invoke the `Search` action method in the `PeopleController` with parameter name as *fanie* and parameter `top` as *5*.

```
[Route("api/{controller}/foo/{action}")]
public class PeopleController
{
    [HttpGet("{name?}")]
    public IActionResult Search(string name, int top)
    {
        // ...
    }
}
```

Notice that the `name` parameter is specified in the route, but not the `id`, and it still maps the `id` parameter from the query parameters. If the `name` parameter weren't part of the route, its value would have tried to be resolved from the query parameters instead.

Likewise, let's look at a route template specified as `[HttpPost("~/api/people")]` and given a `POST` request with parameters like the following:

`POST /api/people?name=Fanie&surname=Reynders`

It will invoke the `Post` action method on `PeopleController`, accepting a `PersonDto` as a complex type with its values mapped from the `name` and `surname` properties in the payload.

```
[HttpPost("~/api/people")]
public IActionResult Post(PersonDto person)
{
// ...
}
```

We can control the default behavior of model binding by explicitly tagging parameters with their origin using the built-in [FromBody], [FromForm], [FromHeader], [FromRoute], and [FromServices] attributes.

Posting raw JSON data to the preceding example will not bind to the person parameter, causing its values to remain null. This is because the raw data is contained in the request body, and to fix this we need to tag the person parameter with [FromBody]. After fixing the code, the following request will invoke the action method properly:

```
POST /api/people

{
    "name":"Fanie",
    "surname":"Reynders"
}
```

Here is the code containing the modification to the parameter for binding request parameters to the request body:

```
[HttpPost("~/api/people")]
public IActionResult Post([FromBody]PersonDto person)
{
    // ...
}
```

Let's say that we need to bind to specific entries in the request header from the following request:

```
POST /api/people
Content-Type: application/json
Access-Token: 1234abcd
ClientId: MyClient1

{
    "name":"Fanie",
    "surname":"Reynders"
}
```

We can simply use the [FromHeader] attribute and apply it to the appropriate action method parameters:

```
[HttpPost("~/api/people")]
public IActionResult Post([FromBody]PersonDto person,
[FromHeader(Name="Access-Token")]string accessToken, [FromHeader]string
clientId)
{
    // ...
}
```

One of the great things about model binding in ASP.NET Core is that it is very customizable. This is quite useful in scenarios where we want to look up some result using data from an incoming request and have the result be bound to a specific parameter type in the action result.

We can build custom model bindings by implementing the IModelBinder interface:

```
public interface IModelBinder
{
    Task BindModelAsync(ModelBindingContext bindingContext);
}
```

For example, let's say we have an API endpoint that receives a *Base64* string of a photo and performs emotion recognition on it. Normally, we would have an action method accept a string parameter as the Base64 content of the photo, then do the logic for retrieving the emotional statistics inside the action.

Custom model binding can be useful in this case to allow us to receive a strongly typed object in the action method containing an object with the emotion statistics instead of a simple string value. Here is a snippet of a class that implements IModelBinder:

```
public class AwesomeModelBinder : IModelBinder
{
    public async Task BindModelAsync(ModelBindingContext bindingContext)
    {
        const string propertyName = "Photo";
        var valueProviderResult = bindingContext.ValueProvider.
        GetValue(propertyName);
        var base64Value = valueProviderResult.FirstValue;
```

```
        if (!string.IsNullOrEmpty(base64Value))
        {
            var bytes = Convert.FromBase64String(base64Value);
            var emotionResult = await GetEmotionResultAsync(bytes);
            var score = emotionResult.First().Scores;
            var result = new EmotionalPhotoDto
            {
                Contents = bytes,
                Scores = score
            };

            bindingContext.Result = ModelBindingResult.Success(result);
        }
        await Task.FromResult(Task.CompletedTask);
    }

    // ...
}
```

The BindModelAsync method retrieves the first value of the Photo property on the model and then converts it to a byte array, which is then passed to the GetEmotionResultAsync function for performing analysis on emotion statistics. The result returned is then used to construct a new EmotionalPhotoDto object containing the photo contents as well as the emotion statistics of the photo. Lastly, the result of the binding context is then successfully set as the value of the EmotionalPhotoDto object.

Here are the contents of the GetEmotionResultAsync function, which uses an HttpClient to do a service call to the emotion API of the Microsoft Cognitive Services REST API to retrieve the emotion statistics of a given image:

```
private static async Task<EmotionResultDto[]> GetEmotionResultAsync(byte[]
byteArray)
{
    var client = new HttpClient();
    client.DefaultRequestHeaders.Add("Ocp-Apim-Subscription-Key",
    <SUBSCRIPTION_KEY>); //
```

```
var uri = "https://<SUBSCRIPTION_LOCATION>.api.cognitive.microsoft.com/
emotion/v1.0/recognize?";
using (var content = new ByteArrayContent(byteArray))
{
    content.Headers.ContentType = new MediaTypeHeaderValue("applicati
    on/octet-stream");
    var response = await client.PostAsync(uri, content);
    var responseContent = await response.Content.ReadAsStringAsync();
    var result = JsonConvert.DeserializeObject<EmotionResultDto[]>
    (responseContent);
    return result;
}
}
```

This function returns the response as an array of EmotionResultDto, which looks like the following:

```
public class EmotionResultDto
{
    public EmotionScoresDto Scores { get; set; }
}

public class EmotionScoresDto
{
    public float Anger { get; set; }
    public float Contempt { get; set; }
    public float Disgust { get; set; }
    public float Fear { get; set; }
    public float Happiness { get; set; }
    public float Neutral { get; set; }
    public float Sadness { get; set; }
    public float Surprise { get; set; }
}
```

On the controller, we have a Post action receiving a parameter of type
EmotionalPhotoDto, which looks like the following:

```
[ModelBinder(typeof(AwesomeModelBinder))]
public class EmotionalPhotoDto
{
    public byte[] Contents { get; set; }
    public EmotionScoresDto Scores { get; set; }
}
```

Notice that the EmotionalPhotoDto class is decorated with the ModelBinder attribute
to map it to the AwesomeModelBinder. After running the application, we use Postman to
send a request to the endpoint, as demonstrated in Figure 5-4.

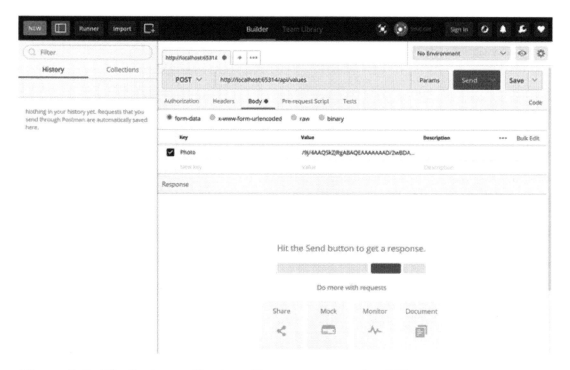

Figure 5-4. *The Postman client sending a request to the API*

When the request is fired, we notice that the parameter expected in the Post action is now properly bound by the emotion statistics of the given photo. Figure 5-5 shows a breakpoint that is being hit, confirming our custom model binding is working as expected.

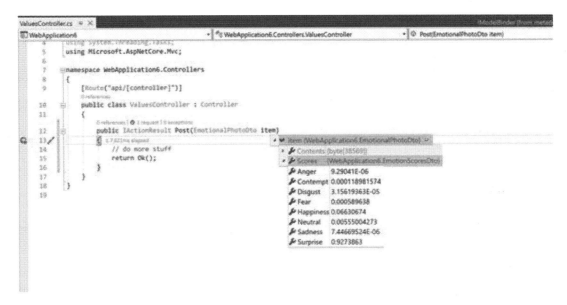

Figure 5-5. *The breakpoint is hit, showing the bound parameter*

If you don't like using ModelBinder attributes on classes, you could make use of a model-binder provider. All you need to do is implement IModelBinderProvider:

```
public class AwesomeModelBinderProvider : IModelBinderProvider
{
    public IModelBinder GetBinder(ModelBinderProviderContext context)
    {
        if (context.Metadata.ModelType == typeof(EmotionalPhotoDto))
        {
            return new BinderTypeModelBinder(typeof(AwesomeModelBinder));
        }

        return null;
    }
}
```

When the provider runs, it returns the appropriate model binder for a specific model type. All that is left to do is to tell ASP.NET Core MVC about this provider; then, there's no more need to make use of the ModelBinder attributes.

```
public void ConfigureServices(IServiceCollection services)
{
    services.AddMvc(options =>
    {
        options.ModelBinderProviders.Insert(0,
        new AwesomeModelBinderProvider());
    });
}
```

Following model binding, the concept of model validation refers to the validation of data before it is used for further processing. Inside ASP.NET Core, validation is simplified using validation attributes that are built right in for convenience. Applying validation using these attributes simply requires us to decorate the appropriate properties on a class that requires validation. ASP.NET Core MVC will take care of the rest when the model is evaluated for validity. The following sample DTO class shows how we can implement simple validation on a Person resource:

```
public class PersonDto
{
    [Required]
    public int Id { get; set; }
    [Required, MaxLength(20)]
    public string FirstName { get; set; }
    [MinLength(5)]
    public string LastName { get; set; }
    [EmailAddress]
    public string Email { get; set; }
    [Url]
    public string BlogUrl { get; set; }
    [Range(1, 5)]
    public int Level { get; set; }
}
```

The attributes used in the preceding code are pretty much self-explanatory.
To validate a certain object, we can check for the `ModelState.IsValid` property, which is provided by the `ControllerBase` class. Here's an example of how a model is validated:

```
public IActionResult Post([FromBody] PersonDto item)
{
    if (ModelState.IsValid)
    {
        // do more stuff
        return Ok();
    }
    else
    {
        return BadRequest(ModelState);
    }
}
```

Tip   When using POCO controller classes, the `ModelState` property is not available directly, but can be explicitly acquired by injecting an `IActionContextAccessor` constructor parameter and reading the `ModelState` property from the `ActionContext` provided.

When invoking the `Post` endpoint with the following invalid data in the request payload:

```
POST /api/values
Content-Type: application/json

{
    "blogUrl":"http:\\www.example.org"
}
```

we will get the following response back because `ModelState.IsValid` evaluated as `false`:

```
{
    "Level": [
        "The field Level must be between 1 and 5."
    ],
    "BlogUrl": [
        "The BlogUrl field is not a valid fully-qualified http, https, or
        ftp URL."
    ],
    "FirstName": [
        "The FirstName field is required."
    ]
}
```

Generally, the validation attributes provided in the framework are enough, but we can most definitely create our own validation rules if required. Custom validation can be done in two ways—namely, as validation attributes by inheriting the custom attribute from `ValidationAttribute` or by having the model implement the `IValidatableObject` interface.

Let's say we want to build a custom validation attribute that checks if the value starts with a capital letter. The following code shows how we can achieve that by creating a class that inherits from `ValidationAttribute` and overrides the `IsValid` function:

```
public class StartsWithCapitalLetterAttribute : ValidationAttribute
{
    protected override ValidationResult IsValid(object value,
    ValidationContext validationContext)
    {
        if (value?.ToString()[0] != value?.ToString().ToUpper()[0])
        {
            return new ValidationResult("Value must start with capital
            letter");
        }
        return ValidationResult.Success;
    }
}
```

Now we can decorate the applicable string properties with a `StartsWithCapitalLetter` attribute. Doing the same validation logic, but without the use of attributes, requires us to have the model implement the `IValidatableObject` interface. Here is an extract of the `PersonDto`:

```
public class PersonDto: IValidatableObject
{
    //...

    private bool StartsWithCaps(string value)
    {
        return !string.IsNullOrWhiteSpace(value) && value[0].Equals(value.
        ToUpper()[0]);
    }
    public IEnumerable<ValidationResult> Validate(ValidationContext
    validationContext)
    {
        const string message = "Value must start with capital letter";
        var results = new List<ValidationResult>();
        if (!StartsWithCaps(FirstName))
        {
            yield return new ValidationResult(message,new[] {
            nameof(FirstName) });
        }
        if (!StartsWithCaps(LastName))
        {
            yield return new ValidationResult(message, new[] {
            nameof(LastName) });
        }
    }
}
```

Model binding and model validation are both fundamental elements of ensuring that APIs work correctly in ASP.NET Core and provide huge benefits in terms of the abstraction, scalability, and maintainability of our code.

Filters

Just like middleware, *filters* in ASP.NET Core MVC provide a mechanism to execute code before and after specific stages in the pipeline. Filters have their own sub-pipelines that contain filters that run in a particular order. The filters are grouped into five types. Figure 5-6 shows an overview of the pipeline in context with filters.

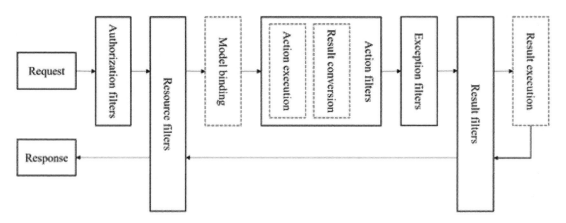

Figure 5-6. *The request pipeline when interacting with filters*

Authorization filters always run first, and their role is to determine if the user in the HTTP context has sufficient privileges for accessing the current request. They can short-circuit a request to return a specific result and implement either the IAsyncAuthorizationFilter or IAsyncAuthorizationFilter interface.

Resource filters run just after the authorization filters and can run logic before and after the rest of the pipeline. They run just before the model-binding process and can perform work to implicate a model's state. With resource filters, it's also possible to short-circuit a request, and they implement either the IAsyncResourceFilter or IResourceFilter interface.

Before and after an action method is executed, **action filters** immediately run and can manipulate the request and response. Action filters implement the IAsyncActionFilter or IActionFilter interfaces.

In the event of unhandled exceptions, **exception filters** are used to apply policies to exceptions not handled before any output is written to the response; these filters implement either the IAsyncExceptionFilter or IExceptionFilter interface.

Result filters run immediately before results are executed and only run when the action method has completed successfully without any errors. Result filters implement either the IAsyncResultFilter or IResultFilter interface.

Filters can be explicitly applied as attributes or globally registered inside the Startup class. Before we create an action filter, let's investigate the signatures of IAsyncActionFilter and IActionFilter:

```
public interface IAsyncActionFilter : IFilterMetadata
{
    Task OnActionExecutionAsync(ActionExecutingContext context,
    ActionExecutionDelegate next);
}

public interface IActionFilter : IFilterMetadata
{
    void OnActionExecuted(ActionExecutedContext context);
    void OnActionExecuting(ActionExecutingContext context);
}
```

Note   Filters should be implemented using either the synchronous or the asynchronous version of the interfaces because the framework first checks for the implementation of the asynchronous version, then for the synchronous version. The asynchronous filters always take precedence over the synchronous filter implementations.

Now, let's implement an action filter so we can understand filters better via a practical example. The action filter that we will build will assign the timestamp in the route value collection to the current timestamp when the request is processed. The action method will also have access to this timestamp variable from its parameters via model binding, which it will use in its response. When the action is finished, before the result is rendered, a new header, X-EXPIRY-TIMESTAMP, will be added to the response headers and will have the value of the original timestamp plus one hour.

Here are the implementations of both the synchronous and asynchronous styles:

```
public class TimestampFilter : IActionFilter, IAsyncActionFilter
{
    public void OnActionExecuting(ActionExecutingContext context)
    {
        context.ActionDescriptor.RouteValues["timestamp"] = DateTime.Now.
        ToString();
    }

    public void OnActionExecuted(ActionExecutedContext context)
    {
        var ts = DateTime.Parse(context.ActionDescriptor.
        RouteValues["timestamp"])
            .AddHours(1)
            .ToString();
        context.HttpContext.Response.Headers["X-EXPIRY-TIMESTAMP"] = ts;
    }

    public async Task OnActionExecutionAsync(ActionExecutingContext
    context, ActionExecutionDelegate next)
    {
        this.OnActionExecuting(context);
        var resultContext = await next();
        this.OnActionExecuted(resultContext);
    }
}
```

The OnActionExecuting method runs before the action is executed, and the
OnActionExecuted method runs after the action method has been executed. Notice
that we are utilizing the synchronous implementation from the asynchronous code in
OnActionExecutionAsync. To register the filter to apply globally to all actions, we need to
add it to the Filters collection on the MvcOptions:

```
public void ConfigureServices(IServiceCollection services)
{
    services.AddMvc(options =>
    {
        options.Filters.Add(typeof(TimestampFilter));
    });
}
```

To be able to apply our filter explicitly to only some action methods, we need to inherit the TimestampFilter class from Attribute and optionally rename it to TimestampFilterAttribute:

```
public class TimestampFilterAttribute : Attribute, IActionFilter,
IAsyncActionFilter
{
    //...
}
```

The preceding code will allow us to decorate the applicable action methods as a TimestampFilterAttribute attribute:

```
[TimestampFilter]
public string Get(string timestamp)
{
    return $"Request received at {timestamp}";
}
```

The mechanism of filters allows for the code to be extremely reusable and decoupled in logical execution layers.

Formatting Responses

As you may have noticed during this chapter, the return type of choice used in action methods is IActionResult, which is not necessary per se, but is considered a best practice because responses are not limited to only one specific type, as they can either succeed or fail.

To explicitly force output of a specific type, we can replace the `IActionResult` with concrete types like, for example, `IEnumerable<T>`, which will then fall back to the default output formatter to render the response. Furthermore, forcing the output as a specific type can be accomplished by using concrete action results like `JsonResponse` for outputting JSON or `ContentResponse` for plain text. Another way of forcing a particular output format is to make use of the `[Produces(...)]` filter, which can be applied to a global, controller, or action scope.

In RESTful services, *content negotiation* is the process of having the client specify the expected format of the output using a specific media-type value passed in the `Accept` header. ASP.NET Core MVC implements a JSON formatter by default, but also supports other formats when they are passed, given that they are correctly registered within the framework at startup.

Web browsers may supply `Accept` headers containing many formats, as well as wildcards. When a request is coming from a web browser, ASP.NET Core MVC will ignore the `Accept` header by default and respond with the standard configured format. This behavior is to keep things a bit more consistent across the board but can be overridden by explicitly setting the `RespectBrowserAcceptHeader` to `true` in the `MvcOptions`.

Content negotiation makes it possible to serve responses from the same action method in different formats. To add XML formatting to our API, we can simply register the XML input and output serialization by adding the XML serializer formatters when adding MVC to the services collection:

```
services.AddMvc().AddXmlSerializerFormatters();
```

We can control supporting specific input or output formatters by registering them in the `MvcOptions`:

```
services.AddMvc(options =>
{
    options.OutputFormatters.Add(new XmlSerializerOutputFormatter());
});
```

When we want content negotiation to handle content types that are not supported by the default JSON, XML, or plain text formatters, we can build custom formatters to handle special media-type formats. In the following example, `PeopleController` delivers an array of people on its `Get` action method:

```
[Route("api/[controller]")]
public class PeopleController : Controller
{
    //...

    public IActionResult Get()
    {
        IEnumerable<Person> result = people;
        return Ok(result);
    }
}
```

If we also wanted to support the *comma-delimited values* (CSV) format, we could create a class that implements the `OutputFormatter` abstract class, like the following:

```
public class CsvOutputFormatter : OutputFormatter
{
    private const string delimiter = ",";
    private const string contentType = "text/csv";
    public CsvOutputFormatter()
    {
        SupportedMediaTypes.Add(MediaTypeHeaderValue.Parse("text/csv"));
    }

    protected override bool CanWriteType(Type type) => type.
GetInterfaces().Contains(typeof(System.Collections.IEnumerable));

    public async override Task WriteResponseBodyAsync(OutputFormatter
WriteContext context)
    {
        var type = context.Object.GetType();
        Type itemType;
```

```
if (type.GetGenericArguments().Length > 0)
{
    itemType = type.GetGenericArguments()[0];
}
else
{
    itemType = type.GetElementType();
}

var stringWriter = new StringWriter();
var header = string.Join(",", itemType.GetProperties().Select
(x => x.Name));
stringWriter.WriteLine(header);

foreach (var item in (IEnumerable<object>)context.Object)
{
    var values = item.GetType().GetProperties().Select(pi => new {
    Value = pi.GetValue(item, null)});

    var valueLine = string.Empty;

    foreach (var val in values)
    {
        if (val.Value != null)
        {
            valueLine = string.Concat(valueLine, val.Value.
            ToString(), delimiter);
        }
        else
        {
            valueLine = string.Concat(valueLine, string.Empty,
            delimiter);
        }
    }
    stringWriter.WriteLine(valueLine);
}
```

```
    var streamWriter = new StreamWriter(context.HttpContext.Response.
    Body);
    await streamWriter.WriteAsync(stringWriter.ToString());
    await streamWriter.FlushAsync();
  }
}
```

Breaking down the preceding bits, we assign *text/csv* as a supported media type inside the constructor of the class. The `CanWriteType` property evaluates if the response is eligible to be converted to CSV. In this case, we assume any result type of `IEnumerable` is eligible.

The `WriteResponseBodyAsync` method does the heavy lifting for constructing the CSV output. The first thing it does is determine the properties of the type it is working with, and then it writes the names of each of those properties as the first line to a `StringWriter`, separated by a comma.

Next, it loops through each item in the collection and tries to resolve their values as a string before writing a comma-separated line to the `StringWriter`. Lastly, it uses a `StreamWriter` to write the string value of the `StringWriter` to the `Response` body.

We should not forget to register this output formatter in the `MvcOptions`:

```
services.AddMvc(options =>
{
    options.OutputFormatters.Add(new CsvOutputFormatter());
});
```

Now when we specify *text/csv* as the `Accept` header in the request to the People API endpoint, we should get the response formatted as CSV.

Application Parts

In ASP.NET Core MVC, each feature of an application is added as an *application part*, which is an abstraction over its resources. By using application parts, we make it possible to discover external components to be used in our application that can even be located in a separate assembly.

Let's assume we have a compiled class library that contains a specific controller called `PeopleController`, which returns a list of people names and is situated within a particular folder on the server. We can make use of the `AddApplicationPart` extension method to add application parts from a given assembly during runtime.

Here's an example configuration of an application that imports all MVC bits from an external assembly from a specific folder on disk:

```
public void ConfigureServices(IServiceCollection services)
{
    var assembly = Assembly.LoadFile(@"C:\folder\mylib.dll");
    services.AddMvc()
            .AddApplicationPart(assembly);
}
```

As this application does not directly contain any controllers, when we run it the magic starts to happen when it manages to invoke action methods originated from specified external locations.

Tip   Application parts not only work for controllers but for other features of ASP. NET Core MVC, like `TagHelpers` and `ViewComponents`, as well.

Wrapping Up

What an exciting chapter this was! After learning how the MVC pattern works, we got introduced to the new MVC framework in ASP.NET Core as well as its features in comparison to its predecessors.

We learned all about the MVC middleware pipeline, including controllers and actions, before moving on to more advanced topics, such as model binding, model validation, and filters. We also gained useful insights into how to leverage the power of convention to have MVC bend to our needs.

In the last sections, we covered how responses are formatted and saw how easy it is to create a custom formatter for outputting CSV data. Lastly, we got a brief overview of application parts, which allow us to import specific features into our application from external sources.

This chapter pretty much sums up ASP.NET Core MVC from an API perspective, and although there is far more to learn about this excellent framework, we will move on to the next chapter, where we will be discussing the configuration model of ASP.NET Core.

CHAPTER 6

The Configuration Model

There's a saying that goes: *"Don't code hard, hardcode instead."* Terrible, I know. Almost all applications have configuration data. Some of them are neatly saved in a configuration file, and others are just hardcoded in a quick and dirty fashion. By using configuration, we make our code much more reusable and can quickly alter the way it works without our having to think about it.

Configuration data should live outside the application. If you feel the urge to hardcode something, stop and think about the impact it may have on the scalability of the application in the future. When we separate the configuration from the application, it allows us to deploy the same code to do different things in different environments.

As .NET developers, we should be familiar with the good old `app.config` and `web.config` files, which offer a mechanism for a specific configuration for each application. ASP.NET Core is no different, but with a much better mechanism for storing and providing configuration data. In fact, the new configuration model in ASP.NET Core is much more simplified, flexible, and extendable. Compared to its predecessors, it sets the bar quite high. In laymen's terms, it is just awesome.

ASP.NET Core provides a configuration API for working with configurations in web apps that is based on a collection of name-value pairs. Configuration data can be read during runtime from multiple sources and are grouped into a multi-level hierarchy.

In this chapter, we will focus on understanding the basic concept of configuration in ASP.NET Core and how to leverage the provided API to read environment-specific configuration data from multiple sources into strongly typed objects.

95

© Fanie Reynders 2018
F. Reynders, *Modern API Design with ASP.NET Core 2*, https://doi.org/10.1007/978-1-4842-3519-5_6

Basic Configuration

Consider the following JSON file that resides in the root directory and is called awesomeConfig.json; it contains some arbitrary configuration data:

```
{
  "foo": "value of foo",
  "bar": "value of bar",
  "baz": {
      "foo": "Hello world"
  }
}
```

We can use this configuration file inside an ASP.NET Core application by creating an IConfigurationRoot that utilizes a ConfigurationBuilder:

```
public class Program
{
    public static IConfigurationRoot Configuration { get; set; }
    public static void Main(string[] args)
    {
        var builder = new ConfigurationBuilder()
            .SetBasePath(Directory.GetCurrentDirectory())
            .AddJsonFile("awesomeConfig.json");
        Configuration = builder.Build();

        foreach (var item in Configuration.AsEnumerable())
        {
            Console.WriteLine($"Key: {item.Key}, Value: {item.Value}");
        }

        Console.ReadKey();
    }
}
```

In the preceding example, we create a new ConfigurationBuilder that loads the awesomeConfig.json file from the current directory using the AddJsonFile extension method. Calling Build on the builder outputs an instance of IConfigurationRoot, which implements IConfiguration, allowing us to enumerate through its key-value pairs. Figure 6-1 shows the output of the executed code.

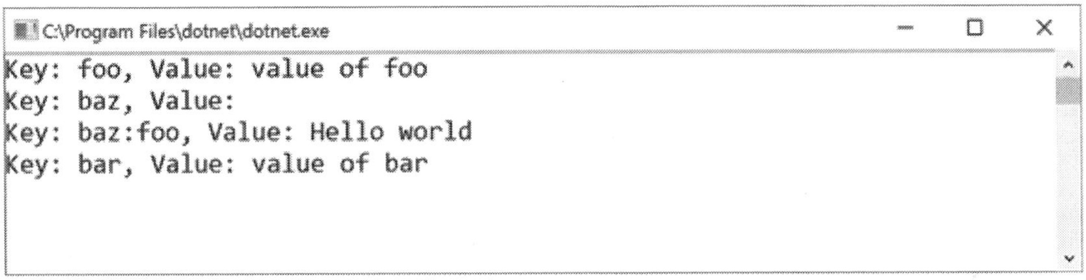

Figure 6-1. *Example code that reads configuration data from a file*

Notice that the awesomeConfig.json file contains hierarchical data but is flattened inside the IConfiguration as simple key-value pairs. To read out the values from IConfiguration, we can simply refer to them by key:

```
Console.WriteLine($"Foo: {Configuration["foo"]}");
Console.WriteLine($"Bar: {Configuration["bar"]}");
Console.WriteLine($"Baz:Foo: {Configuration["baz:foo"]}");
```

The hierarchical value of foo inside baz can be referred to by using the colon (:) character as a separator. As the configuration file can contain multiple levels of hierarchy, it is a better idea to group similar settings using sections:

```
var bazSection = Configuration.GetSection("baz");
Console.WriteLine($"Baz:Foo: {bazSection ["foo"]}");
```

When working with multiple configuration files at the same time, configuration data is loaded in the same order in which it's specified, so the latest values override any previous ones with the same key. For example, given the following files -

Contents of awesomeConfig.json:

```
{
  "foo": "value of foo",
  "bar": "value of bar",
```

```
  "baz": {
    "foo": "Hello world"
  }
}
```

Contents of awesomeConfig2.json:

```
{
  "baz": {
    "foo": "Hello Universe"
  }
}
```

we can override specific configurations by loading another file containing the new configuration values to take precedence over the previous ones. The following code snippet shows how configuration data can be overridden by loading data from multiple files:

```
var builder = new ConfigurationBuilder()
    .SetBasePath(Directory.GetCurrentDirectory())
    .AddJsonFile("awesomeConfig.json")
    .AddJsonFile("awesomeConfig2.json");
```

Figure 6-2 shows the output after running the application with configuration data loaded from awesomeConfig.json and awesomeConfig2.json. Note that the original values from awesomeConfig.json are persisted and only the ones specified in awesomeConfig2.json are overriding the original ones.

Figure 6-2. *Output of an application using inherited and overridden configurations*

Configuration Providers

A configuration can be loaded from many different sources containing many different formats. Configuration providers are responsible for passing the configuration in a specific format from a pre-defined source to the configuration model of ASP.NET Core.

ASP.NET Core ships with default configuration providers out of the box, allowing a configuration to be loaded from files (JSON, XML, and INI formats), command-line arguments, environmental variables, in-memory .NET objects, encrypted user secret stores, the Azure Key Vault, and custom providers that we can create.

The following example shows how we can load a configuration from multiple sources and formats supported by ASP.NET Core:

```
public static void Main(string[] args)
{
    var someSettings = new Dictionary<string, string>()
    {
        { "poco:key1","value 1" },
        { "poco:key2","value 2" }
    };
    var builder = new ConfigurationBuilder()
        .SetBasePath(Directory.GetCurrentDirectory())
        .AddJsonFile("awesomeConfig.json")
        .AddXmlFile("awesomeConfig.xml")
        .AddIniFile("awesomeConfig.ini")
        .AddCommandLine(args)
        .AddEnvironmentVariables()
        .AddInMemoryCollection(someSettings)
        .AddUserSecrets("awesomeSecrets")
        .AddAzureKeyVault("https://awesomevault.vault.azure.net/",
        "<clientId>", "<secret>");

    Configuration = builder.Build();

    // ...
}
```

Figure 6-3 shows the contents of the file sources loaded by the `AddJsonFile`, `AddXmlFile`, and `AddIniFile` extension methods.

```
{
    "jsonSettings": {
        "key1": "value 1",
        "key2": "value 2"
    }
}
```

```
<?xml version="1.0" encoding="utf-8" ?>
<configuration>
    <XmlSettings>
        <Key1>Value 1</Key1>
        <Key2>Value 2</Key2>
    </XmlSettings>
</configuration>
```

```
[iniSettings]
key1=value 1
key2=value 2
```

Figure 6-3. *Example configuration in JSON, XML, and INI formats*

More settings can be loaded into the application from optional command-line arguments. When running the application via the CLI, we can execute the following command from the command prompt:

```
$ dotnet run --cli:key1="Value 1" --cli:key2="Value 2"
```

The preceding code will load the configuration into a section called `cli` containing values for `key1` and `key2` as shown in Figure 6-4.

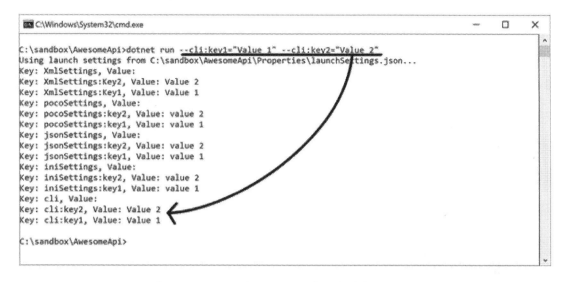

Figure 6-4. *Output showing a configuration loaded from command-line arguments*

The AddEnvironmentVariables method loads in all the environmental variables available on the current environment as key-value entries in the IConfiguration collection. Doing this means that we can access an environment variable by using its key on the IConfiguration object. Calling AddInMemoryCollection will simply add whatever IEnumerable<KeyValuePair<string,string>> is passed to it as part of the configuration.

User secrets are used mainly for development purposes to prevent the check-in of sensitive files into source control that contain required configuration data. When calling AddUserSecrets, a configuration file called secrets.json in JSON format is loaded from a specific location on disk (outside source control) for a particular secretId. User secrets will be loaded from the following locations on each operating system:

- Windows: %APPDATA%\microsoft\UserSecrets\<*userSecretsId*> \secrets.json

- Linux: ~/.microsoft/usersecrets/<*userSecretsId*>/secrets.json

- Mac: ~/.microsoft/usersecrets/<*userSecretsId*>/secrets.json

---

Note   User secrets are not encrypted and should not be used for storing sensitive information, as they are intended for development purposes only.

We can manually add or modify values in the secret.json file located on each platform, but can also make use of the *Secret Manager CLI* tool. To install the Secret Manager tool, we need to open the .csproj file and add a new DotNetCliToolReference element to one of the ItemGroup elements:

```
<Project Sdk="Microsoft.NET.Sdk.Web">
  <PropertyGroup>
    <TargetFramework>netcoreapp2.0</TargetFramework>
  </PropertyGroup>
  <ItemGroup>
    <PackageReference Include="Microsoft.AspNetCore.All" Version="2.0.0" />
    <DotNetCliToolReference Include="Microsoft.Extensions.SecretManager.
    Tools" Version="2.0.0" />
  </ItemGroup>
</Project>
```

After saving the .csproj file and running a quick dotnet restore, the Secret Manager will be installed and ready for use. To add a setting to user secrets, we run the following command from the CLI:

```
$ dotnet user-secrets --id awesomeSecrets set key1 "Value 1"
```

Note   We are using the --id option in the preceding CLI command to specify which user secret the setting applies to. We can skip this by adding a UserSecretsId element containing the secret ID in a PropertyGroup inside the .csproj file.

We can get a list of secrets for a specific user secret by executing the following command from the CLI:

```
$ dotnet user-secrets --id awesomeSecrets list
```

When we need to access sensitive information as a configuration in our application, we can make use of the *Azure Key Vault* to store confidential data securely in the cloud. To obtain access to an Azure Key Vault from our application, and to load it into the configuration collection, we can call AddAzureKeyVault and then pass in the *vault URL*, *client ID*, and *client secret*.

Instead of passing hard-coded Azure Vault connection information, we can make use of the ConfigurationBuilder to surface available settings containing connection information for accessing the Azure Key Vault. Here's an example of the modified code that uses the `ConfigurationBuilder` to read out connection information from the AzureKeyVault section instead of hard-coding it:

```
public static void Main(string[] args)
{
    // ...
    var builder = new ConfigurationBuilder()
        .SetBasePath(Directory.GetCurrentDirectory())
        .AddJsonFile("awesomeConfig.json")
        .AddXmlFile("awesomeConfig.xml")
        .AddIniFile("awesomeConfig.ini")
        .AddCommandLine(args)
        .AddEnvironmentVariables()
        .AddInMemoryCollection(someSettings)
        .AddUserSecrets("awesomeSecrets");

    var config = builder.Build();
    builder.AddAzureKeyVault(config["AzureKeyVault:url"], config["AzureKey
    Vault:clientId"], config["AzureKeyVault:secret"]);

    Configuration = builder.Build();

    //...
}
```

The `ConfigurationBuilder` can call `Build` at any time necessary for consumption, which can come in handy when we need to use it in itself.

If you are familiar with the previous configuration model of .NET, the following example `web.config` file will be familiar:

```
<?xml version="1.0" encoding="utf-8" ?>
<configuration>
  <connectionStrings>
    <add name="db1" connectionString="Server=myServerAddress;Database=
    myDataBase1;Trusted_Connection=True;"/>
    <add name="db2" connectionString="Server=myServerAddress;Database=
    myDataBase2;Trusted_Connection=True;"/>
  </connectionStrings>
```

```
<appSettings>
  <add key ="setting1" value="value1"/>
  <add key ="setting2" value="value2"/>
</appSettings>
</configuration>
```

To be able to use this configuration file within an ASP.NET Core application, we call
AddXmlFile to use the built-in XML file provider, but if the configuration contains more
than one add element per section, it will break when running the application, as shown
in Figure 6-5.

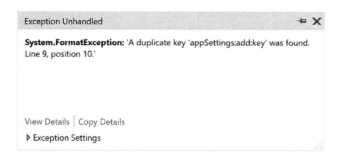

Figure 6-5. An example exception when a duplicate key is found

We are getting this error because there are duplicate keys found in the configuration
dictionary. We can solve this by creating a custom configuration provider by
implementing IConfigurationProvider and IConfigurationSource.

Let's create a new class named AwesomeConfigurationProvider and inherit it
from the ConfigurationProvider base class, which is built in to ASP.NET Core. We
also need to implement the IConfigurationSource interface to be able to pass it to the
configuration builder.

```
public class AwesomeConfigurationProvider : ConfigurationProvider,
IConfigurationSource
{
    public IConfigurationProvider Build(IConfigurationBuilder builder)
    {
        return this;
    }
}
```

When the Build function is executed, it will simply return an instance of itself, which is of type IConfigurationProvider. The provided ConfigurationProvider base class does most of the default plumbing for us; we just need to override its Load method:

```
public class AwesomeConfigurationProvider: ConfigurationProvider,
IConfigurationSource
{
    private readonly string fileName;
    public AwesomeConfigurationProvider(string fileName)
    {
        this.fileName = fileName;
    }
    public override void Load()
    {
        using (var fs = new FileStream(fileName, FileMode.Open))
        {
            var doc = XDocument.Load(fs);
            var connectionStrings = doc.Root.Descendants()
                .Where(e => e.Name.Equals(XName.Get("connectionStrings")))
                .Descendants(XName.Get("add")).Select(e =>
                    new KeyValuePair<string,
                    string>($"connectionStrings:{e.Attribute(XName.
                    Get("name")).Value}", e.Attribute(XName.
                    Get("connectionString")).Value));
            var appSettings = doc.Root.Descendants()
                .Where(e => e.Name.Equals(XName.Get("appSettings")))
                .Descendants(XName.Get("add")).Select(e =>
                    new KeyValuePair<string, string>($"appSettings:{e.
                    Attribute(XName.Get("key")).Value}", e.Attribute(XName.
                    Get("value")).Value));

            Data = connectionStrings.Union(appSettings).ToDictionary(e=>e.
            Key, e=>e.Value);
        }
    }
    // ...
}
```

The implementation is quite simple. We make use of *LINQ-to-XML* to load the file stream into an XDocument. Thereafter, we read out all the connectionString and appSetting elements and select a flat key-value structure using the values provided in each of the add elements. The keys contained in the key-value structures are in *section:key* format. Lastly, we assign the key-value collections to the Data dictionary, which is a property in the ConfigurationProvider base class.

Now we can pass an instance of AwesomeConfigurationProvider to the configuration builder. We do this by creating a new extension method that extends an IConfigurationBuilder:

```
public static class AwesomeConfigurationExtensions
{
    public static IConfigurationBuilder AddLegacyXmlConfiguration(this
IConfigurationBuilder configurationBuilder, string path)
    {
        return configurationBuilder.Add(new
        AwesomeConfigurationProvider(path));
    }
}
```

This allows us to neatly specify a configuration source by invoking the AddLegacyXmlConfiguration extension method, which adds a new instance of IConfigurationProvider to the configuration builder:

```
var builder = new ConfigurationBuilder()
    .SetBasePath(Directory.GetCurrentDirectory())
    .AddLegacyXmlConfiguration("web.config");
```

Strongly Typed Configuration

Although reading configuration data directly from IConfigurationRoot or IConfiguration is great, it still would be way better to address the configuration using a strongly typed object. Let's take a look at the same sample JSON file awesomeConfig. json used earlier in this chapter:

```
{
  "foo": "value of foo",
  "bar": "value of bar",
```

```
  "baz": {
    "foo": "Hello world"
  }
}
```

We create a POCO class called AwesomeOptions that represents the structure of the configuration file:

```
public class AwesomeOptions
{
    public string Foo { get; set; }
    public string Bar { get; set; }
    public BazOptions Baz { get; set; }
    public class BazOptions
    {
        public string Foo { get; set; }
    }
}
```

By modifying the original code, we can use the Bind extension method on IConfiguration to bind the values from the key-value collection to a strongly typed POCO instance:

```
public static void Main(string[] args)
{
    var builder = new ConfigurationBuilder()
        .SetBasePath(Directory.GetCurrentDirectory())
        .AddJsonFile("awesomeConfig.json");

    var awesomeOptions = new AwesomeOptions();
    builder.Build().Bind(awesomeOptions);

    Console.WriteLine($"Foo: {awesomeOptions.Foo}");
    Console.WriteLine($"Bar: {awesomeOptions.Bar}");
    Console.WriteLine($"Baz.Foo: {awesomeOptions.Baz.Foo}");

    Console.ReadKey();
}
```

Now, let's apply this in a proper scenario within the application Startup class. It turns out that there is an even more elegant way of working with strongly typed configurations. Given a standard MVC application, we have an application startup like the following:

```
public class Startup
{
    public Startup()
    {
        var builder = new ConfigurationBuilder()
            .SetBasePath(env.ContentRootPath)
            .AddJsonFile("awesomeConfig.json");

        Configuration = builder.Build();
    }

    public IConfigurationRoot Configuration { get; set; }

    public void ConfigureServices(IServiceCollection services)
    {
        services.AddMvc();
    }

    public void Configure(IApplicationBuilder app)
    {
        app.UseMvc();
    }
}
```

To add a strongly typed configuration, we need to call the Configure extension method on IServiceCollection inside the ConfigureServices method and specify the type as AwesomeOptions:

```
public void ConfigureServices(IServiceCollection services)
{
    services.AddMvc();
    services.Configure<AwesomeOptions>(Configuration);
}
```

This will allow the injection of IOptions<AwesomeOptions> from anywhere in the application. Here's an example of AwesomeController using AwesomeOptions options:

```
public class AwesomeController
{
    private readonly AwesomeOptions awesomeOptions;
    public AwesomeController(IOptions<AwesomeOptions> awesomeOptions)
    {
        this.awesomeOptions = awesomeOptions.Value;
    }

    //...
}
```

Calling Configure not only works with the given ConfigurationRoot, but also works quite well with configuration sections:

```
public void ConfigureServices(IServiceCollection services)
{
    //...

    services.Configure<AwesomeOptions.BazOptions>(Configuration.
    GetSection("baz"));
}
```

This will bind a specific section of a configuration to a strongly typed POCO class, which can be injected anywhere in the application. For example:

```
public class AwesomeController
{
    private readonly AwesomeOptions.BazOptions bazOptions;
    public AwesomeController(IOptions<AwesomeOptions.BazOptions> bazOptions)
    {
        this.bazOptions = bazOptions.Value;
    }

    //...
}
```

Working with Changes

Now that we know all the great things about creating beautiful configurations inside ASP.NET Core, it is important to understand that configuration data may change during runtime, and we need our application to react to changes accordingly.

When working with file-based configurations in ASP.NET Core, we can specify that the configuration model should be reloaded whenever there are changes to the configuration data, and this is as easy as setting the `ReloadOnChange` property to `true`:

```
var builder = new ConfigurationBuilder()
    .SetBasePath(env.ContentRootPath)
    .AddJsonFile(config =>
    {
        config.Path = "awesomeConfig.json";
        config.ReloadOnChange = true;
    });
```

Wherever `IConfigurationRoot` and `IConfiguration` are used, they will reflect the latest configuration data pulled from the file that has potentially changed, except when `IOptions<T>` is used. Even if the file changes and configuration model are updated via the file provider, the instance of `IOptions<T>` will still contain the original values.

To have the configuration data automatically reload the strongly typed `IOptions<T>` class as well, we need to use `IOptionsSnapshot<T>` instead:

```
public class AwesomeController

    private readonly AwesomeOptions awesomeOptions;
    public AwesomeController(IOptionsSnapshot<AwesomeOptions>
    awesomeOptions)
    {
        this.awesomeOptions = awesomeOptions.Value;
    }

    //...
}
```

Using `IOptionsSnapshot<T>` has very minimal overhead and allows us to reload strongly typed POCO classes whenever the configuration data in the original file changes.

Wrapping Up

We have come to the end of yet another chapter where we learned exciting new things about ASP.NET Core. In this chapter, we explored the basics of how the configuration model works and how we can quickly load configuration data in any supported format from multiple different sources.

We covered the eight built-in configuration providers that ship with ASP.NET Core and learned how they could be used in conjunction with each other to override specific values. In this chapter, we also learned how to build a custom configuration provider that loads the settings used in legacy systems straight into the configuration model.

Another key takeaway of this chapter was binding the configuration model to strongly typed POCO classes that can be injected and used anywhere in an application. We also saw how easy it is to refresh the configuration model whenever something changes within the configuration files.

In the next chapter, we will learn all about logging, which helps us gain useful insights into our ASP.NET Core applications.

CHAPTER 7

Logging and Error Handling

Application logging plays a crucial role in tracking and identifying issues that may surface as well as in providing useful insights on the workflow processes of solutions. When things go wrong, one of the first sources to look at is the application's log. Depending on the number of details that are logged, each entry represents an action that occurred at a specific date and time.

Logs can contain system-generated events as well as events explicitly defined by the developer and are usually grouped into categories like errors, informational, and warning. Application logs are application specific, hence the name, and do not often include OS-specific events.

In this chapter, we will focus on understanding how logging can benefit applications and help us extract useful information about why certain things happen. We will be introduced to ASP.NET Core's logging API and learn how to quickly get started with adding logging functionality to any ASP.NET Core application.

During this chapter, we will work with the different parts of a log entry and learn how to correctly group log entries to keep similar items together. We will learn about log filtering and how to log certain types of entries in specific scenarios and environments.

We will cover the six built-in logging providers of ASP.NET Core and how to use them, as well as some third-party logging providers that are available. At the end of the chapter, we also will learn about error handling and how to catch and handle application exceptions.

113

© Fanie Reynders 2018
F. Reynders, *Modern API Design with ASP.NET Core 2*, https://doi.org/10.1007/978-1-4842-3519-5_7

Adding Logging

Logging can be used anywhere in ASP.NET Core, and to create a log we merely need to inject an ILogger object that was previously registered in the DI container. Before logging can be used, the specific logging configuration first needs to be added to the host.

Looking at the ILogger interface, it exposes a Log method that we can use to write a specific type of entry and exception to the configured logging providers:

```
public interface ILogger
{
    IDisposable BeginScope<TState>(TState state);
    bool IsEnabled(LogLevel logLevel);
    void Log<TState>(LogLevel logLevel, EventId eventId, TState state,
Exception exception, Func<TState, Exception, string> formatter);
}
```

We can use the Log method on the Ilogger—for example, logging a simple, informative string:

```
logger.Log(LogLevel.Information, 0, typeof(object), null,
(type,exception)=> "Hello world");
```

As we noticed, doing this every time we want to make a log entry can become quite tedious and will make our code very unreadable. Fortunately, there are extension methods available for logging specific levels of log entries; they are LogCritical for critical logs, LogDebug for logging debug information, LogError for logging exceptions, LogInformation for logging informative entries, LogTrace for logging trace entries, and LogWarning for logging any warning entries. We will go deeper into log levels and severity in the next section.

Let's take a look at the most basic example of an application with a host using Kestrel and a separate Startup class:

```
using Microsoft.AspNetCore.Hosting;
using Microsoft.AspNetCore.Builder;
using Microsoft.AspNetCore.Http;
using Microsoft.Extensions.Logging;
```

```
public class Program
{
    public static void Main(string[] args)
    {
        new WebHostBuilder()
            .UseKestrel()
            .UseStartup<Startup>()
            .ConfigureLogging(logging =>
            {
                logging.AddConsole();
            })
            .Build()
            .Run();
    }

    public class Startup
    {
        public void Configure(IApplicationBuilder app, ILogger<Startup>
        logger)
        {
            app.Run(async (context) =>
            {
                logger.LogInformation("This is awesome!");
                await context.Response.WriteAsync("Hello World!");
            });
        }
    }
}
```

Investigating the preceding code, we see that the host is configured with logging to the console window. In the Configure method of the Startup class, a logger parameter type of ILogger<out TCategoryName> is injected, where TCategoryName can be any type, and usually the class of where the log entry is added from. Figure 7-1 shows that the log entries are logged to the console window when running the application and invoking the default endpoint.

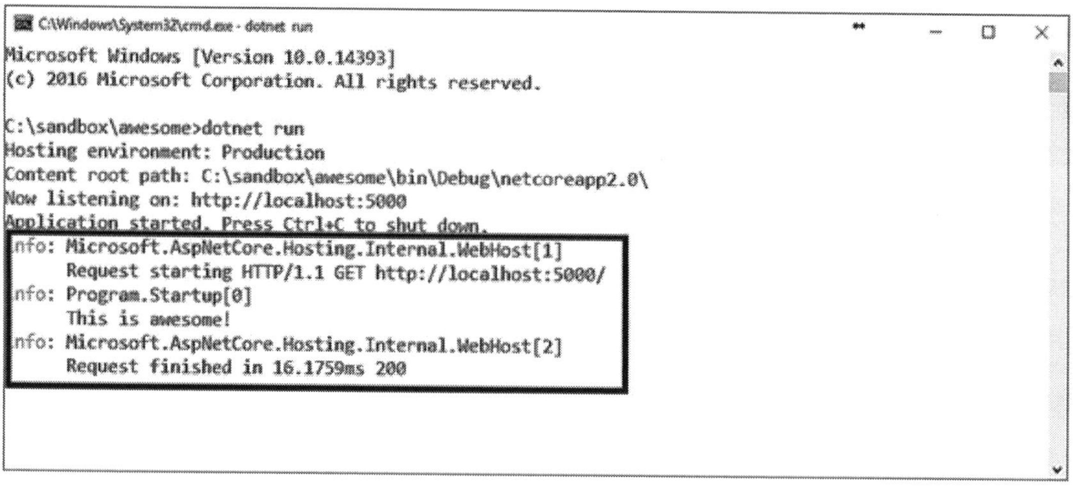

Figure 7-1. *The output of an application with console logging*

What we see in the console is that three informational events occurred. The framework logged when the request started and finished, and the application code logged *"This is awesome!"* upon invocation of the default endpoint.

Log Anatomy

When creating logs, we need to map it to a category string, which is used during the output of the entry. As we saw in the previous section, a log is typically created to be used inside a specific class, which is thus the category.

It is possible to write log entries to many categories within a given class. By making use of an ILoggerFactory, we can create a logger *on-the-fly*, bound to a specific group. Altering our initial code, let's add logging to other parts of the Startup class:

```
public class Startup
{
    private readonly ILoggerFactory loggerFactory;

    public Startup(ILoggerFactory loggerFactory)
    {
        this.loggerFactory = loggerFactory;
        var constructorLogger = loggerFactory.CreateLogger("Startup.ctor");
        constructorLogger.LogInformation("Logging from constructor!");
    }
```

```
public void Configure(IApplicationBuilder app)
{
    var configureLogger = loggerFactory.CreateLogger("Startup.
    Configure");
    configureLogger.LogInformation("Logging from Configure!");
    app.Run(async (context) =>
    {
        var logger = loggerFactory.CreateLogger("Startup.Configure.Run");
        configureLogger.LogInformation("Logging from app.Run!");
        await context.Response.WriteAsync("Hello World!");
    });
}
}
```

An `ILoggerFactory` is injected into the constructor and used to create an `ILogger` wherever a specific logger is required. In the preceding code, three loggers are created for three parts of the class. Figure 7-2 shows the output of the updated code when running and invoking the default endpoint.

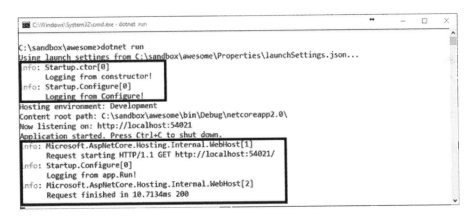

Figure 7-2. *Output of the updated code using multiple loggers*

Ideally, we need to stick to one category per class to keep things simple. In the previous example, we notice a number *zero* in *block brackets* ([0]), which is the identifier of the event. Because we never specified an event ID, it defaults to 0. Using event IDs can help us to classify the log entries as belonging to related parts of the application.

Let's now get rid of the multiple loggers and revert to injecting the ILogger<Startup>, but this time into the constructor, and also making use of proper event IDs:

```
public class Startup
{
    private readonly ILogger logger;

    public Startup(ILogger<Startup> logger)
    {
        this.logger = logger;
        logger.LogInformation(1000, "Logging from constructor!");
    }
    public void Configure(IApplicationBuilder app)
    {
        logger.LogInformation(1001, "Logging from Configure!");
        app.Run(async (context) =>
        {
            logger.LogInformation(1002, "Logging from app.Run!");
            await context.Response.WriteAsync("Hello World!");
        });
    }
}
```

As seen in Figure 7-3, each event within a category can have a specific event ID tied to it, which we can later map to some friendly string.

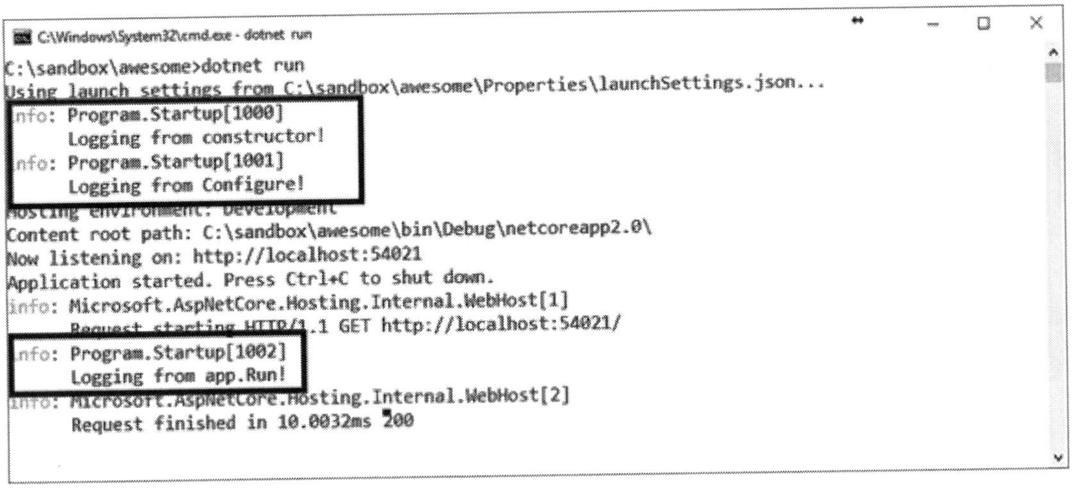

Figure 7-3. *Log entries with event IDs*

In ASP.NET Core, log levels are used to determine the severity of the log entry and are ordered in the following order, from the least to the highest severity:

- **Trace** has the lowest severity of 0 and is only to be used in specific scenarios to provide the developer with valuable information when debugging an issue. As trace log entries may contain sensitive data, this type is disabled by default for the production environment.

- **Debug** entries have a severity of 1 and are used for short-term information during development and debugging. To prevent an overload of information in the logs, these kind of entries are typically disabled for production and enabled on demand whenever an issue is debugged.

- **Information** type entries have a severity of 2 and are mainly used to log the general workflow of an application. Having informative logs is a good thing but can be dangerous if not used correctly, so keeping to this level of severity is entirely up to the developer.

- **Warning** entries have a severity of 3 and are mainly used for unexpected events that occur in the application workflow. Typically, validation and general errors that are handled are commonly classified as a warning.

LOGGING AND ERROR HANDLING

- **Error log** entries have a severity of 4 and are used for any unhandled errors or exceptions within the scope of the application; they indicate a failure inside the current activity, but not application wide.

- As the name suggests, **Critical** entries are reserved for all application-wide failures that require immediate attention and have the highest severity of 5.

- The **None** log level has a severity of 6 and is mainly used for log filtering.

A log entry has a specific message it writes to the logging providers, and this message can be formatted to contain data that are related to the log entry. Let's say we want to log a user's whereabouts with the current date and time. Writing the following code snippet will write a message that contains the current date and time:

```
logger.LogInformation("User {userName} entered at {entryTime}", userName,
DateTime.Now);
```

This will output the following to the log:

```
User Fanie entered at 11/30/2017 15:01:53
```

We could also have used the *Interpolated Strings* feature of C# 6 to format the log entry's variables inline by doing the following:

```
logger.LogInformation($"User {userName} entered at {DateTime.Now}");
```

Although writing it like this increases the readability of the code, it will not send the parameter collection to the logging provider, which may use the parameters as metadata. If we formatted the log entries as in the preceding example, the following sample output of log entries would be the same for humans, but different for machines:

```
User Fanie entered at 11/30/2017 15:01:53
User Steven entered at 11/30/2017 16:08:22
User Andrea entered at 11/30/2017 16:11:53
User Gerald entered at 11/30/2017 16:23:10
User Peter entered at 11/30/2017 16:30:03
User Martin entered at 11/30/2017 16:35:12
```

Let's say we want to find all check-ins after a certain date and time. Searching through the preceding log might become tricky as we would then need to make use of clever wildcard tricks or regular expressions for matching strings.

When we provide the format of the message and the variables separately, the logging provider can make use of the submitted data and store them separately so they can be queried against.

Note   The framework does string formatting in this way to implement semantic or structured logging so that logging providers have more control over the data inside the log entries.

Log entries also can contain an optional exception object that can be used to extend the metadata of the specific entry in the log.

Grouping and Filtering

At times it is necessary to capture more details of a given transaction or process. We can group a set of logical operations with the same log information by using scopes, which are IDisposable objects that result from calling ILogger.BeginScope<TState> and last until they are disposed of. Let's use a scope to group some of the log entries inside the Configure method:

```
public void Configure(IApplicationBuilder app)
{
    app.Run(async (context) =>
    {
        using (logger.BeginScope("This is an awesome group"))
        {
            logger.LogInformation("Log entry 1");
            logger.LogWarning("Log entry 2");
            logger.LogError("Log entry 3");
        }
        await context.Response.WriteAsync("Hello World!");
    });
}
```

121

It is important to point out that the details of scoped logs need to be explicitly enabled on the provider. To do this, we need to set the IncludeScopes property for the provided options object of the provider:

```
public static void Main(string[] args)
{
    new WebHostBuilder()
        .UseKestrel()
        .UseStartup<Startup>()
        .ConfigureLogging(logging =>
        {
            logging.AddConsole(options=>options.IncludeScopes = true);
        })
        .Build()
        .Run();
}
```

Figure 7-4 shows the output of the logs after we've added grouping and enabled scopes on the provider.

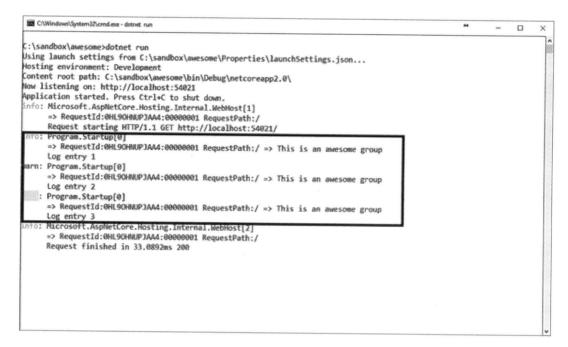

Figure 7-4. *Sample output showing scopes in logs*

It is possible to specify a minimum log-level severity for everything or to enforce a specific filter for a certain provider and category. All logs sent that are below the provided minimum log level aren't sent to the particular logging provider, which means they won't get processed, stored, or displayed.

To set the minimum log level across the board in code, we need to call the SetMinimumLevel function:

```
public static void Main(string[] args)
{
    new WebHostBuilder()
        .UseKestrel()
        .UseStartup<Startup>()
        .ConfigureLogging(logging =>
        {
            logging.AddConsole();
            logging.SetMinimumLevel(LogLevel.Information);
        })
        .Build()
        .Run();
}
```

Tip   To suppress all logs, set the minimum level to LogLevel.None.

Within the ConfigureLogging function, we can also define minimum levels for different scenarios. For example, the following code suppresses all severities for all logs, except for the Default and Program.Startup categories, as they have a minimum level of Error and Critical, respectively:

```
logging
    .SetMinimumLevel(LogLevel.None);
    .AddFilter("Default", LogLevel.Error)
    .AddFilter<ConsoleLoggerProvider>("Program.Startup", LogLevel.Critical);
```

Note   The last filter in the preceding code is specific to the Console logger.

Filters can work both ways, in that we can specify minimum levels and special conditions in order to only show certain severity levels. The following code limits the logging by only showing Warning entries globally and Information entries specific to the Console logger:

```
logging
    .AddFilter(s => s == LogLevel.Warning)
    .AddFilter<ConsoleLoggerProvider>(s => s == LogLevel.Information);
```

We have total control over how and when things are logged. The examples thus far have showed how we could configure log grouping and filtering using code, but we could also make use of the powerful configuration system to abstract all these configurations into a separate file, making it more maintainable.

To integrate with the configuration model, we need to set up the application configuration on the web host and bind it to the logging configuration, like in the following example snippet:

```
public static void Main(string[] args)
{
    new WebHostBuilder()
        .UseKestrel()
        .UseStartup<Startup>()
        .UseContentRoot(Directory.GetCurrentDirectory())
        .ConfigureAppConfiguration((context, config) =>
        {
            config.AddJsonFile("config.json")
        .ConfigureLogging((context, logging) =>
        {
            var config = context.Configuration.GetSection("Logging");
            logging.AddConfiguration(config);
            logging.AddConsole();
        })
        .Build()
        .Run();
}
```

The config.json file will then look something like the following; it excludes all scopes and sets the log filters for each category accordingly:

```
{
  "Logging": {
    "IncludeScopes": false,
    "LogLevel": {
      "Default": "Error"
    },
    "Console": {
      "LogLevel": {
        "Program.Startup": "Critical"
      }
    }
  }
}
```

Different Logging Providers

ASP.NET Core ships with built-in support for six logging providers. So far, we have only used the Console logger to write log output to the console window, but we can easily add more logging providers to work in conjunction with each other.

We already know to add the **Console** logging provider; we can just call the AddConsole function on the ILoggingBuilder.

As developers, we sometimes need to log useful information to the IDE or similar environment, and that is when the **Debug** logger can come in handy. We can add the Debug logger by calling the AddDebug function on the ILoggingBuilder. This provider writes the logging output using the System.Diagnostics.Debug class by using Debug.WriteLine calls.

Note   Linux logs written to the Debug logger will end up in the /var/log/ message path.

To enable logging to an event tracer, we can use the **EventSource** logging provider, which is cross-platform and allows us to log events to *Event Tracing for Windows* (ETW) when running on the Windows operating system. Calling the AddEventSourceLogger function on the ILoggerProvider will set up logging using the EventSource provider.

In cases where we need to log to the Windows Event Log, we can make use of the **EventLog** logging provider, adding it by calling the AddEventLog function on the ILoggingBuilder. Here's an example snippet for logging to the Windows Event Log:

```
logger.AddEventLog(new EventLogSettings
{
    EventLog = new EventLog("AwesomeLog", "AwesomeMachine", "AwesomeApi")
});
```

Note   The code in the example assumes that a log called *AwesomeLog* and log source *AwesomeApi* already exist on a machine with the name *AwesomeMachine*.

The **Trace Listener** provider allows us to log to a variety of trace listeners, such as the TextWriterTraceListener; we can add it by calling the AddTraceSource method on ILoggingBuilder.

Note   The EventLog and Trace Listener providers are Windows-only and require your application to target the full .NET 4.6 framework. If the application targets operating systems other than Windows, one should make use of #if definitions. Read more on targeting multiple platforms here: https://docs.microsoft.com/en-us/dotnet/core/tutorials/libraries.

If an application is deployed to Azure as an app service, it automatically gets configured with the **Azure App Service** logging provider. All that we need to do is turn it on inside the Azure portal. This provider does not affect when we run the application locally and will only work within the Azure environment.

One of the great things about ASP.NET Core is the open source community projects, some of which offer great extensions to the framework. Some of the third-party logging providers out there are *Elmah.IO* (https://github.com/elmahio/Elmah.Io.Extensions.Logging), *JSNLog* (http://jsnlog.com), *Loggr* (https://github.

com/imobile3/Loggr.Extensions.Logging), *NLog* (https://github.com/NLog/
NLog.Extensions.Logging), and *Serilog* (https://github.com/serilog/serilog-
extensions-logging). These logging providers are excellent and allow us to plug it in
and have it work as expected.

Dealing with Exceptions

It is essential that our applications deal with any exception that might occur. This ties in
with the fact that logging is significant for debugging critical issues. As developers, we
tend to be lazy, and looking up problems in a log file isn't always the best solution while
developing.

To help us gain instant insight into why a particular request goes wrong, we can
make use of special developer exception pages provided by ASP.NET Core. They are
HTML-based pages generated by the runtime that encapsulate all the useful information
around the problem, like the stack trace, for instance.

Here's an example snippet of how we can switch on the developer exception pages
inside an ASP.NET Core application:

```
public void Configure(IApplicationBuilder app, IHostingEnvironment env)
{
    if (env.IsDevelopment())
    {
        app.UseDeveloperExceptionPage();
    }
}
```

As we can see, the UseDeveloperExceptionPage function is only called if the
current environment is *Development*. Figure 7-5 shows a typical example of an
ArgumentNullException that is thrown by the server and displayed nicely in a
developer-friendly console.

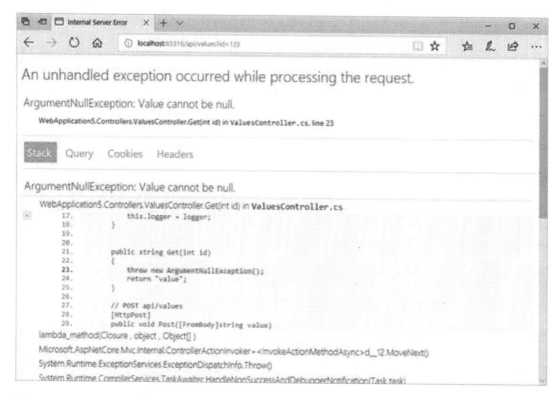

Figure 7-5. *Example of a developer exception page*

Developer exception pages give us useful insights, like the full stack trace that includes a view pointing to the specific line of code in question, the query string collection, any cookies, and the full request headers that were passed.

Note   Developer exception pages must only be enabled for development environments as you don't want sensitive information, like the stack trace, visible on production.

When making a request, the HTTP mechanism always provides a status code with the response. These status codes include the *1xx-series*, which are used for informational purposes, the *2xx-series*, which indicate successful responses, such as 200 OK or 201 Created, the *3xx-series*, which indicate some form of redirection, the *4xx-series* for client errors, like 404 Not Found or 400 Bad Request, and the *5xx-series*, which are server errors, like 500 Internal Server Error.

By default, ASP.NET Core applications do not provide any other details on status codes, but we can enable these details by using the StatusCodePagesMiddleware. We must call the UseStatusPages extension method available on IApplicationBuilder:

```
public void Configure(IApplicationBuilder app)
{
    app.UseStatusCodePages();
}
```

When running the application and invoking an endpoint that does not exist, we will get the following response formatted as plain text:

```
Status code page, status code: 404
```

We can also customize the response to our liking. For example, the following code uses an overload of the UseStatusCodePages function, thus allowing us to write directly to the Response stream:

```
app.UseStatusCodePages(async context =>
{
    context.HttpContext.Response.ContentType = "text/plain";
        await context.HttpContext.Response.WriteAsync(
        $"Awesome Status Page, status code: {context.HttpContext.Response.
StatusCode}");
});
```

Now, when the application hits a Not Found error, the following will be in the response body:

```
Awesome Status Page, status code: 404
```

Note   Although a response body is returned, the status code in the header will still be the appropriate status code as expected.

Wrapping Up

Great! We are at the end of the chapter. So far, we have learned about the importance of application logging and how to add logging to an application using the API provided by ASP. NET Core. We covered the different log severities as well as the various parts of a log entry.

We learned how log entries could be suppressed or explicitly filtered for specific scenarios and environments, as well as how to abstract the logging configuration away from the code by making use of the configuration model.

We briefly went through all the internal and external logging providers that are available right now in the latest version of ASP.NET Core. Lastly, we saw how to make use of developer-friendly exception pages when debugging during the development lifecycle, as well as how to add custom responses to specific response statuses.

In the next chapter, we will turn the knob up a notch and learn all about implementing security for APIs in ASP.NET Core.

CHAPTER 8

Securing APIs

Having APIs everywhere is excellent, but they need to be secure externally as well as internally. Even a small breach has the potential risk of a damaging ripple effect. API security is not limited to authentication or authorization but also includes protecting the underlying infrastructure, like rate limiting to prevent *denial of service* (dos) or *distributed denial of service* (DDoS) attacks. Attackers continuously come up with new and creative ways to breach systems, and it's important to keep on standard and up-to-date with the latest threats out there.

ASP.NET Core offers a wide range of features to help us configure and manage the security of our APIs. The framework provides a rich identity model for securing applications and integrates with third-party identity providers like Facebook or Twitter, as well as offers a mechanism to manage application secrets for communicating with these providers.

In this chapter, we will learn the basics of what authentication and authorization are by clearly understanding the differences between them as well as ways of implementing them in our API applications. We will learn about the ASP.NET Core data-protection stack for storing sensitive data securely and how to enforce secure communication by using a *secure sockets layer* (SSL).

We will end the chapter by implementing *cross-origin resource sharing* (CORS) to prevent cross-domain service calls and rate-limiting in order to prevent DoS as well as DDoS attacks.

Note   The overall scope of this book only covers a subset of all the security features provided by ASP.NET Core, which are focused toward implementing security within the context of API applications.

131

© Fanie Reynders 2018
F. Reynders, *Modern API Design with ASP.NET Core 2*, https://doi.org/10.1007/978-1-4842-3519-5_8

Authentication & Authorization

Before we move on, it is important to understand what authentication and authorization are, as well as what the difference is between them. **Authentication** is the process of verifying the identity of the person or system requesting access to a specific resource, and **authorization** is the process of verifying if the authenticated user has the sufficient rights to do certain things. Think of authentication as the right one has to enter a room, while authorization dictates what one can do once in the room.

The authentication process can be abstracted away from the application and used by other services as well, but the authorization process is typically specific to an application, where specific roles have different permissions.

The HTTP protocol provides a mechanism to negotiate access to a secure resource. Figure 8-1 shows the process of HTTP authentication.

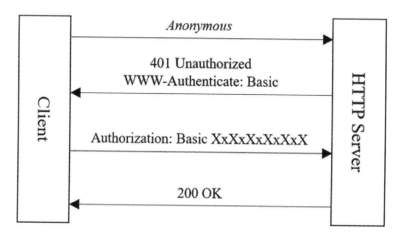

Figure 8-1. *A typical authentication flow*

A standard authentication workflow starts with an anonymous request of a protected resource on the server. The HTTP server handles the request and denies access to the protected resource due to insufficient credentials, then sends a WWW-Authenticate header back indicating the types of authentication schemes that are required. The client sends a request containing an Authorization header, with the value conforming to the particular authentication scheme required. When the server receives the request, it validates the credentials in the Authorization header and lets the request through the pipeline.

The server can provide multiple authentication schemes that the client can choose from for authenticating them. From the flow shown in Figure 8-1, we see that the server is using the `Basic` authentication scheme. Here are some other authentication schemes:

- Although the **Anonymous** scheme cannot be classified as an authentication scheme, it is still an empty scheme that does not contain any authentication information. It is mainly used to grant access to everyone.

- The **Basic** authentication scheme is one of the oldest and previously most commonly used schemes for authenticating users as it provides a simple authentication flow. This scheme requires a string that consists out of a username and password concatenated with a *colon* (:), and then encoded as a Base64 string. For example, a typical `Authorization` header containing a Basic authentication scheme with username *awesomeuser* and password as *awesomepassword* may look like this:

  ```
  Authorization: Basic YXdlc29tZXVzZXI6YXdlc29tZXBhc3N3b3Jk
  ```

Note   The credentials in the Basic authentication scheme are encoded and not encrypted, and are sent over the wire as plain text. Using the Basic authentication scheme to secure resources is not recommended, but it is strongly advised that you consider the use of SSL in the scenario where there is no other choice.

- The **Digest** authentication scheme is a replacement for the Basic authentication scheme. The server sends a random string to the client as a *challenge*. This random string is called a *nonce*. The client authenticates them by sending a hash that contains a username, password, and nonce, as well as potentially other information.

- **Bearer** authentication is among the most popular and more secure authentication schemes around. It works by making use of bearer tokens for accessing *OAuth 2.0*–protected resources. Anyone in possession of a bearer token can gain access to associated resources. Bearer tokens are usually short-lived and expire after a specific point in time. Here's an example of an `Authorization` header containing a Bearer token:

```
Authorization: Bearer eyJ0eXAiOiJKV1QiLCJhbGciOiJIUzI1NiJ9.e30.3u5
UwreDwHRgVR4roifZDnacpsa3hkX5_hqhp6tLnV0
```

- The **NTLM** authentication scheme is short for *NT LAN Manager* and is a challenge–response scheme that is more secure than the Digest scheme. This scheme uses Windows credentials to transform the challenge data, instead of using the encoded credentials.

- The **Negotiate** scheme automatically selects between the NTLM authentication scheme and the *Kerberos* protocol, which is faster than NTLM.

Note   The NTLM and Negotiate authentication schemes are specific to the Windows operating system.

There are a few things to consider when deciding which authentication scheme to go with. When implementing security, think about what you are trying to protect and whether the resource that is being protected *really* needs to be protected. Adding HTTP authentication to the mix adds more overhead to requests and responses, making it less interoperable with clients.

When security is a must, consider an authentication scheme with the right level of protection; the Basic scheme provides the least amount of security and the Negotiate scheme is the strongest.

A server should never provide a `WWW-Authenticate` scheme that it does not support or does not correctly implement to secure a particular resource. Clients ultimately have a choice between the schemes provided by the server.

With ASP.NET Core we have a range of choices of authentication providers with which to implement security. **ASP.NET Core Identity** is a membership system for adding login functionality to applications and provides a mechanism for users to log in to the app with credentials or by using a third party, like Facebook, Twitter, Google, Microsoft, and others.

Note ASP.NET Core Identity is most commonly used with web applications consisting of user interfaces, and not with web APIs. This feature of ASP.NET Core is considered out of scope for this literature.

When hosting applications in the cloud, we can leverage the power of **Azure Active Directory** (AAD) to act as a gatekeeper for protecting secure resources. ASP.NET Core has native integration with AAD by making use of Bearer authentication. Azure also offers **Azure Active Directory B2C (Azure AD B2C)**, which is a cloud identity-management solution for web applications that have a minimal configuration for authenticating against social, enterprise, and local accounts.

Note Read more on Azure AD B2C and explore a sample ASP.NET Core 2.0 implementation here: `https://azure.microsoft.com/en-gb/resources/samples/active-directory-b2c-dotnetcore-webapi`.

There are also great third-party OSS authentication providers available from the community, like *AspNet.Security.OpenIdConnect.Server* (ASOS), *IdentityServer4*, and *OpenIddict*, which are OpenID Connect server frameworks for ASP.NET Core, as well as *PwdLess*, which is a simple and stateless mechanism for authentication in ASP.NET Core without using passwords.

Now that we have a broader understanding of authentication, authorization, and the surrounding technologies, let's implement security on an API by using the Bearer authentication scheme. For this implementation, we will make use of *JSON Web Tokens* (JWTs), which is an open and industry standard for representing claims between parties.

The JWT standard provides a compact and self-contained way to transfer information between two parties as a JSON object. JWTs are signed with an *HMAC* secret or an *RSA* public and private key pair. A JWT consists of three parts, namely a header, a payload, and a signature, and is rendered using the following pseudocode:

```
[X=base64(header)].[Y=base64(payload)].[sign([X].[Y])]
```

The resulting JWT token is a string consisting of the three parts separated by a dot (.). The first two parts are Base64-encoded strings of the header and payload sections in the JSON object, and the last part is a combination of the first two Base64 strings, separated by a dot (.) and signed.

135

Figure 8-2 explains the typical flow when using JWT tokens with the Bearer authentication scheme.

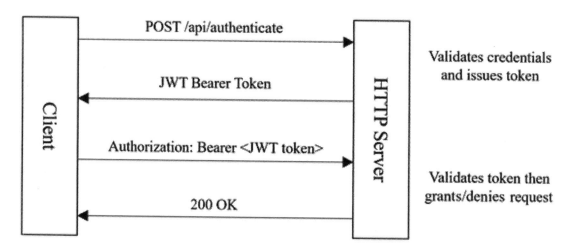

Figure 8-2. *A typical flow of Bearer authentication using JWT*

Note   You can read more on JSON Web Tokens here:
`https://jwt.io/introduction`.

The following example is based on the standard Web API template in ASP.NET Core and contains the *Values* API. To start implementing Bearer authentication on this API, we need to add the authentication middleware to ASP.NET Core and configure it to use JWT Bearer authentication. Here is an excerpt from the `Startup` class:

```
public class Startup
{
    //...

    public void ConfigureServices(IServiceCollection services)
    {
        services
            .AddAuthentication(JwtBearerDefaults.AuthenticationScheme)
            .AddJwtBearer(options =>
            {
```

```
            var serverSecret = new SymmetricSecurityKey(Encoding.UTF8.
            GetBytes(Configuration["JWT:ServerSecret"]));
            options.TokenValidationParameters = new
            TokenValidationParameters
            {
                IssuerSigningKey = serverSecret,
                ValidIssuer = Configuration["JWT:Issuer"],
                ValidAudience = Configuration["JWT:Audience"]
            };
        });

    services.AddMvc();
}

public void Configure(IApplicationBuilder app)
{
    app.UseAuthentication();
    app.UseMvc();
}
}
```

When adding the authentication middleware by calling AddAuthentication, we configure the default authentication scheme to be Bearer. By further configuring the authentication, we call the AddJwtBearer function and specify JwtBearerOptions, where the IssuerSigningKey, ValidIssuer, and ValidAudience are assigned from the values sourced in the appSettings.json configuration file.

Inside the Configure function, we need to remember to call UseAuthentication, which puts everything in place for the authentication flow.

Note   The AddAuthentication and UseAuthentication methods are called before AddMvc and UseMvc to handle authentication early in the pipeline.

Before running the application, we need to decorate the ValuesController with the [Authorize] attribute to have it protected using our authentication mechanism.

After running the application and attempting to request to /api/values, the following response is returned:

```
HTTP/1.1 401 Unauthorized
...
WWW-Authenticate: Bearer
```

As we can see, the status is 401, which means we are not authorized for access, and the WWW-Authenticate response header hints that we should use the Bearer scheme.

Let's now add the endpoint for issuing the JWT token. We create a new Controller called AuthenticateController and add the JWT-generation logic inside the Post action. Here, we want to verify the client credentials to generate a JWT token.

Credentials are to be posted to the /api/authenticate endpoint using Basic security, with the Authorization header set to the Base64-encoded value of awesome-user:awesome-password.

The following code snippet shows the contents of the AuthenticateController class:

```
[Route("api/authenticate")]
public class AuthenticateController: Controller
{
    //...
    public IActionResult Post()
    {
        var authorizationHeader = Request.Headers["Authorization"].First();
        var key = authorizationHeader.Split(' ')[1];
        var credentials = Encoding.UTF8.GetString(Convert.
        FromBase64String(key)).Split(':');
        var serverSecret = new SymmetricSecurityKey(Encoding.UTF8.GetBytes
        (Configuration["JWT:ServerSecret"]));

        if (credentials[0] == "awesome-username" && credentials[1] ==
        "awesome-password")
        {
            var result = new
            {
                token = GenerateToken(serverSecret)
            };
```

```
        return Ok(result);
    }
    return BadRequest();
}
//...
```

After the Authorization header is parsed, the credentials are validated, and if they are valid, we then call the GenerateToken function, which generates the JWT token using the given server secret sourced from the appSettings.json configuration file:

```
private string GenerateToken(SecurityKey key)
{
    var now = DateTime.UtcNow;
    var issuer = Configuration["JWT:Issuer"];
    var audience = Configuration["JWT:Audience"];
    var identity = new ClaimsIdentity();
    var signingCredentials = new SigningCredentials(key,
    SecurityAlgorithms.HmacSha256);
    var handler = new JwtSecurityTokenHandler();
    var token = handler.CreateJwtSecurityToken(issuer, audience, identity,
    now, now.Add(TimeSpan.FromHours(1)), now, signingCredentials);
    var encodedJwt = handler.WriteToken(token);
    return encodedJwt;
}
```

The GenerateToken method uses multiple variables, like the issuer and audience from the configuration file, and generates a new JWT token that is valid for one hour. After running the application, we can invoke the following request:

```
POST /api/authenticate HTTP/1.1
...
Authorization: Basic YXdlc29tZS11c2VybmFtZTphd2Vzb211LXBhc3N3b3Jk
```

The following response will then be returned:

```
HTTP/1.1 200 OK
{
    "token": "..."
}
```

Now that we have a valid JWT token, let's try it out by executing the same request to a protected resource as we did earlier in this section, but this time it will send the Bearer token in the `Authorization` header:

```
GET /api/values HTTP/1.1
...
Authorization: Bearer ...
```

Executing the preceding request will return a 200 OK response containing the expected results inside the response body.

Now that we are more familiar with adding Bearer authentication, we will shift our focus from securing protected resources to protecting sensitive data.

Protecting Sensitive Data

Sometimes it is necessary to store sensitive data, and we need a way to securely protect the contents thereof using a reliable and robust mechanism because the storing mechanism might not be as secure. The data-protection APIs provided by Windows are great for securing sensitive data on desktop applications but are not suitable for web applications.

The ASP.NET Core data-protection stack offers a long-term replacement for the old cryptography model used in previous versions of ASP.NET and is designed to align better with modern security requirements out of the box.

Note   The API provided by the data-protection stack is not officially intended for the indefinite storage of secured data but can be used to do so depending on the scenario and the discretion of the developer. Other technologies, like Azure Rights Management, are more suitable for indefinite storage of sensitive data as they support stronger key-management capabilities.

Let's look at a basic example of how we can protect sensitive data within an ASP.NET Core application. Here, we have a simple program that endlessly asks for the input of sensitive data and outputs both the protected and unprotected versions of the original input:

```
using System;
using Microsoft.AspNetCore.DataProtection;
using Microsoft.Extensions.DependencyInjection;

public class Program
{
    public static void Main(string[] args)
    {
        var services = new ServiceCollection()
            .AddDataProtection()
            .Services.BuildServiceProvider();

        var protecterProvider = services.GetService<IDataProtectionProvider>();
        var protector = protecterProvider.CreateProtector("AwesomePurpose");

        while (true)
        {
            Console.Write($"Type something sensitive: ");
            var input = Console.ReadLine();
            var protectedInput = protector.Protect(input);
            Console.WriteLine($"Protected: {protectedInput}");
            var unprotectedInput = protector.Unprotect(protectedInput);
            Console.WriteLine($"Unprotected: {unprotectedInput}");
            Console.WriteLine();
        }
    }
}
```

The preceding code shows the use of the data-protection API in its simplest form. To make use of the data-protection API, we need to add it to the IServicesCollection by calling the AddDataProtection extension method. Doing this will allow the injection of an IDataProtectionProvider instance.

We use the `IDataProtectionProvider` instance to create an `IDataProtector` for a specific purpose, given a purpose string. The purpose string doesn't necessarily have to be a secret, as it is used to create a unique data-protection mechanism for specifying a purpose.

Tip   Multiple purposes and sub-purposes can be defined for an `IdataProtector`.

After reading the user input, we call the `Protect` method on the `IDataProtector` instance that creates an obfuscated string from the original data. Calling the `Unprotect` method on the instance will result in a new string that is equal to the initial unprotected input.

Figure 8-3 shows the results of four attempts to protect and unprotect the "Something secure" string.

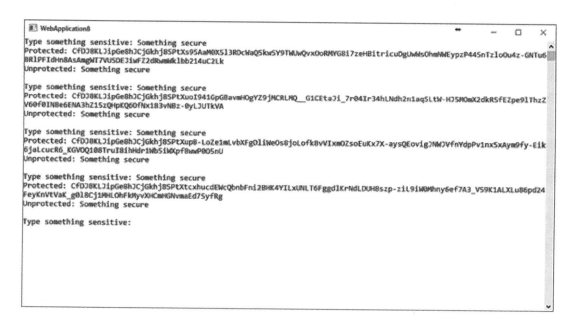

Figure 8-3. *A sample program for protecting and unprotecting a given string*

An interesting observation is that the same string is protected four times, each with different protected payloads, but when they are unprotected, it equates to the original string.

Another neat feature is the ability to have protected data expire after a specified time. By using a special `IDataProtector` we can limit the validity of any previously protected payload. The `ITimeLimitedDataProtector` inherits from an `IDataProtector` and allows for expiration to be specified for a specific data-protection action.

Let's alter our code a bit to see how we can enable data-protection expiration for a message after ten seconds:

```
public static void Main(string[] args)
{
    var services = new ServiceCollection()
        .AddDataProtection()
        .Services.BuildServiceProvider();

    var protecterProvider = services.GetService<IDataProtectionProvider>();
    var protector = protecterProvider.CreateProtector("AwesomePurpose").
    ToTimeLimitedDataProtector();

    DateTimeOffset expiryDate;

    Console.Write($"Type something sensitive: ");
    var input = Console.ReadLine();
    var protectedInput = protector.Protect(input, TimeSpan.FromSeconds(10));

    while (true)
    {
        try
        {
            Console.Clear();
            Console.WriteLine($"Protected: {protectedInput}");
            var unprotectedInput = protector.Unprotect(protectedInput,
            out expiryDate);
            Console.WriteLine($"Unprotected: {unprotectedInput}");
            Console.WriteLine($"This message will self-destruct in
            {(expiryDate - DateTime.Now).Seconds} second(s).");
        }
        catch (CryptographicException ex)
        {
```

```
        Console.WriteLine(ex.Message);
    }
    finally
    {
        Thread.Sleep(1000);
    }
    }
}
```

We call the `ToTimeLimitedDataProtector` extension method on the protector to create an `ITimeLimitedDataProtector`, which will allow us to specify a `Timespan` value for how long the protected payload data is valid until it expires. Upon expiration, a `CryptographicException` is thrown. Figure 8-4 shows the output of the program after adding support for data-protection expiration.

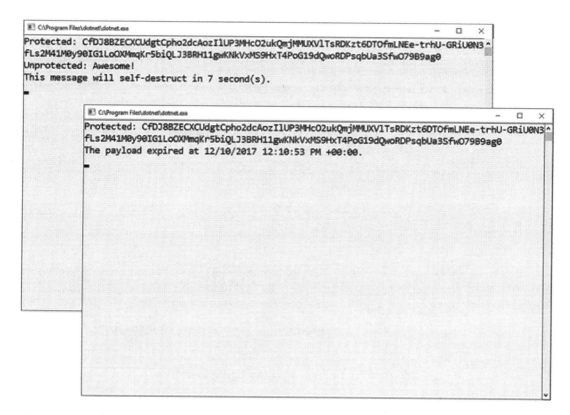

Figure 8-4. *Protected payload expiration*

Enforcing SSL

So far, we've covered how to gain access to secured resources as well as how to protect the data of applications, but what about the communication between the client and the server? A *secure sockets layer* (SSL) is a protocol for transmitting private data via the web. By enforcing SSL, we add a layer of security to our solution to make it less vulnerable to attacks.

Tip   It is recommended to enforce SSL in the overall communication between the components of applications as it will reduce the risk of *man-in-the-middle attacks* (MITM). Read more about MITM here: `https://en.wikipedia.org/wiki/Man-in-the-middle_attack`.

When using MVC, we can apply the [RequireHttps] attribute at all the places where SSL is required. Enforcing SSL on a global level is a security best practice and can be achieved by adding a new instance of a RequireHttpsAttribute to the MVC filters collection:

```
public void ConfigureServices(IServiceCollection services)
{
    services.Configure<MvcOptions>(options =>
    {
        options.Filters.Add(new RequireHttpsAttribute());
    });
    //...
}
```

The RequireHttpsAttribute will require the use of the SSL protocol when making requests to the service. To automatically redirect all requests via HTTPS, we need to implement a rewriter to redirect all requests to their subsequent HTTPS variants. The HTTPS rewriter can be implemented by making use of the AddRedirectToHttps extension method:

```
public void Configure(IApplicationBuilder app)
{
    //...
```

```
    var options = new RewriteOptions()
        .AddRedirectToHttps();

    app.UseRewriter(options);
}
```

Note   To use SSL, one will need to have a valid certificate that is issued by a certificate authority. It is possible to get a free SSL certificate from Let's Encrypt; visit them here: `https://letsencrypt.org`.

Cross-origin Requests

Most browsers have a built-in security mechanism that prevents web pages from making AJAX requests to other domains that are different from the current website or application. This restriction is called a same-origin policy and helps to protect websites against malicious access to sensitive data from other sites.

In the modern API landscape, chances of having different domains between the components of applications are pretty good, and sometimes there is a need to let sites make cross-origin domain calls to various web APIs. *Cross-origin resource sharing* (CORS) is a W3C standard that solves this problem by allowing the relaxation of the same-origin policy.

By using CORS, a server can explicitly allow specific cross-origin requests, and it's much safer than previous techniques were that tried to solve the cross-origin problem. An origin of a request is the combination of the scheme, host, and port. The following example endpoint URLs have identical origins:

```
https://api.awesome.com/customers
https://api.awesome.com/customers/2/orders
https://api.awesome.com/orders/2/history
```

The first endpoint URL could have the following different origins:

```
https://api.awesome.com/customers
http://api.awesome.com/customers
http://api.awesome.com:8080/customers
http://awesome.com/api/customers
```

CORS doesn't just limit origins, but can also be configured to allow or deny HTTP methods and HTTP headers.

Browsers that support CORS set special headers automatically for cross-origin requests, which are validated by the server implementing CORS on the back-end. If the validation fails, it will cause the AJAX request to fail, and thus will not make the response available to the client, even if the response was successful.

In ASP.NET Core, we can implement CORS by registering the CORS middleware in the ConfigureServices method and enabling it globally in the Configure method of a Startup class. The following example adds CORS to an application that only allows requests from http://awesome.com:

```
public class Startup
{
    public void ConfigureServices(IServiceCollection services)
    {
        services.AddCors();

        //...
    }

    public void Configure(IApplicationBuilder app)
    {
        app.UseCors(config => config.WithOrigins("http://awesome.com"));

    //...
    }
}
```

Note   When specifying the origin URL, remember to exclude the possible trailing slash (/) character, as this will cause the origin validation to fail.

147

It is important to enable CORS before any other defined components in the request pipeline in order for CORS to properly take effect. We can also create CORS policies that will apply in different places in our application, as shown in the code snippet here:

```
public void ConfigureServices(IServiceCollection services)
{
    services.AddCors(options=>
    {
        options.AddPolicy("AwesomePolicy", builder => builder.
        WithOrigins("http://awesome.com"));
    });

    //...
}
```

We can then use a specific CORS policy on the entire application using the CORS middleware:

```
public void Configure(IApplicationBuilder app)
{
    app.UseCors("AwesomePolicy");

    //...
}
```

If we are using MVC, we could implement CORS even further on different levels. For example, here's a code snippet showing the AwesomePolicy CORS policy being used globally within MVC by adding the CorsAuthorizationFilterFactory to the global filter collection:

```
public void ConfigureServices(IServiceCollection services)
{
    services.AddMvc();
    services.Configure<MvcOptions>(options =>
    {
        options.Filters.Add(new CorsAuthorizationFilterFactory
        ("AwesomePolicy"));
    });
}
```

Alternatively, we could also add CORS per controller level and action level by using the EnableCorsAtrribute:

```
[Route("api/[controller]")]
[EnableCors("AwesomePolicy")]
public class AwesomeController : Controller
{
    [EnableCors("AnotherAwesomePolicy")]
    public IEnumerable<string> Get()
    {
        //...
    }

    [DisableCors]
    public string Post()
    {
        //...
    }

    //...
}
```

In the preceding code snippet, the AwesomePolicy is applied to the whole AwesomeController class, and furthermore the Get action method also contains the AnotherAwesomePolicy CORS policy. To exempt a CORS policy on a particular level, we can use the DisableCorsAttribute, as shown in the Post action method.

Request Rate Limiting

When an application processes too many requests at once, it can cause a system failure or even have a negative impact on the underlying infrastructure. We can prevent potential down-time by implementing request rate limiting on our application, which will also help protect against DoS and DDoS attacks.

Implementing a request rate limiter is as simple as adding strategic middleware in the request pipeline to validate incoming requests and then accept or deny them, depending on the outcome of the validation process. Here's an example of simple request rate limiting, which limits requests to five requests every thirty seconds, as implemented in the AwesomeRateLimiterMiddleware class:

```
public class AwesomeRateLimiterMiddleware
{
    private const int limit = 5;
    private readonly RequestDelegate next;
    private readonly IMemoryCache requestStore;

    public AwesomeRateLimiterMiddleware(RequestDelegate next, IMemoryCache
    requestStore)
    {
        this.next = next;
        this.requestStore = requestStore;
    }

    public async Task Invoke(HttpContext context)
    {
        var requestKey = $"{context.Request.Method}-{context.Request.Path}";
        int hitCount = 0;
        var cacheEntryOptions = new MemoryCacheEntryOptions()
        {
            AbsoluteExpiration = DateTime.Now.AddSeconds(30)
        };

        if (requestStore.TryGetValue(requestKey, out hitCount))
        {
            if (hitCount < limit)
            {
                await ProcessRequest(context, requestKey, hitCount,
                cacheEntryOptions);
            }
            else
            {
```

```
                context.Response.Headers["X-Retry-After"] =
                cacheEntryOptions.AbsoluteExpiration?.ToString();
                await context.Response.WriteAsync("Quota exceeded");
            }
        }
        else
        {
            await ProcessRequest(context, requestKey, hitCount,
            cacheEntryOptions) ;
        }
    }

    private async Task ProcessRequest(HttpContext context, string
    requestKey, int hitCount, MemoryCacheEntryOptions cacheEntryOptions)
    {
        hitCount++;
        requestStore.Set(requestKey, hitCount, cacheEntryOptions);
        context.Response.Headers["X-Rate-Limit"] = limit.ToString();
        context.Response.Headers["X-Rate-Limit-Remaining"] = (limit -
        hitCount).ToString();
        await next(context);
    }
}
```

By studying the preceding class, we can see that when the middleware is invoked, an attempt is made to read the number of requests for a specific request key, which can be any unique string value. In this scenario, the key is a combination of the HTTP method and the request path.

If a value is found, a check is performed to see if the number of requests amount is larger than five. If the number of requests is larger than five, it immediately sends a response back indicating that the rate limit has been exceeded. If the number of requests is still smaller than five, then it allows the request through the pipeline and increases the number of requests for that specific request in the in-memory request store.

As a best practice, statistics of the request rate limiting are sent with the response by using a response header X-Rate-Limit that indicates what the current rate limit is, as well as a response header X-Rate-Limit-Remaining, which is a value indicating how many requests are available for the particular request until requests are rate limited. Also, when rate limiting kicks in, a specific X-Retry-After header is sent that indicates when the request can be retried without its being rate limited.

To use the AwesomeRateLimiterMiddleware middleware in our application, we need to make sure to add an implementation of IMemoryCache to the services collection and to register the middleware as early as possible in the request pipeline:

```
public class Startup
{
    public void ConfigureServices(IServiceCollection services)
    {
        services.AddMemoryCache();
    }

    public void Configure(IApplicationBuilder app)
    {
        app.UseMiddleware<AwesomeRateLimiterMiddleware>();
        app.Run(async (context) =>
        {
            await context.Response.WriteAsync("Hello World!");
        });
    }
}
```

Now, when we run our application and execute the request for more than five times within a time span of thirty seconds, we will get a response indicating that the current request is rate limited.

Tip   The preceding code is intended for conceptual purposes only. There are plenty of great third-party request limiting implementations available in the community. One such implementation is *AspNetCoreRateLimit* by Stefan Prodan and is available here: https://github.com/stefanprodan/AspNetCoreRateLimit.

Wrapping Up

We've reached the end of yet another chapter of the journey of modern API design in ASP. NET Core. After learning all about authentication and authorization, we implemented basic JWT authentication to protect our application from unauthorized entry.

We learned about the ASP.NET data-protection stack and how we can leverage it to protect and unprotect payloads of data for specific purposes. We also covered how to enforce SSL to help guarantee secure communication between the client and the server.

We ended the chapter by covering more advanced concepts of security, like using CORS for cross-origin requests and request rate limiting to help prevent the system from being overloaded with requests during a potential attack.

In the next chapter, we will continue our journey of modern API design by taking a look at more concepts and technologies to help implement fantastic APIs.

CHAPTER 9

Bells & Whistles

By now we've covered many essential aspects critical to building modern APIs; however, sometimes there is a requirement to add extra value to the solution proposition to make it stand out above the rest.

As mentioned previously, developers are ultimately the end-users of our APIs, and the onus is on us to deliver the best possible experience to them while they use our API solution. This chapter is focused on some of the additional technologies and other concepts that can help accelerate the adoption and usability experience of APIs.

After learning about managing the API state with HATEOAS, we will discover the use of versioning within our APIs and cover different ways of implementing a versioned API. In this chapter, we will also delve into the use of other tools and frameworks, such as Swagger, for developing, interacting with, and documenting APIs, as well as GraphQL, for providing a unified querying experience.

Note There are, of course, many other add-ons we could implement to make our APIs great. The ones detailed in this chapter are just a subset, but are definitely among my favorite.

HATEOAS

As we know by now, one of the constraints of REST is the notion of being completely *stateless*. To refresh our memories, this means that when a request is sent by the client to the server, it should contain all the information needed to process the request without relying on the server for tracking the interaction state.

155

© Fanie Reynders 2018
F. Reynders, *Modern API Design with ASP.NET Core 2*, https://doi.org/10.1007/978-1-4842-3519-5_9

Hypermedia As The Engine Of Application State (HATEOAS) is a constraint of the stateless application that allows a REST client to have no prior knowledge of how to interact with the server beyond a general understanding of hypermedia provided by the API.

It works by having a client enter a REST application using a fixed URL and then be provided with further functionality that is discovered as the interaction between the client and server continues. This communication between client and server is shown in Figure 9-1.

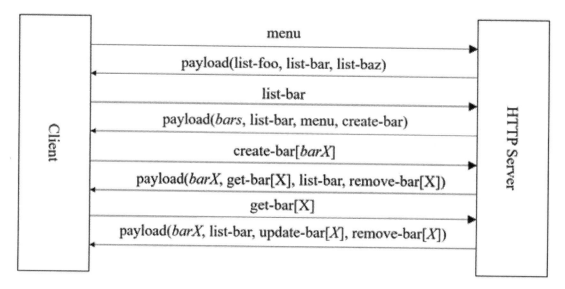

Figure 9-1. *An example set of interactions with a server implementing HATEOAS*

In the preceding figure, the client makes an initial request to the server to get the possible functionality and receives back a payload containing available actions for the current state. The client then requests a list of bars by invoking the URL of the provided list-bar action and receives back a payload containing a collection of bars, as well as further steps that can be invoked for the current state of the response.

If the client requests that a new bar be created by invoking the create-bar action URL, it receives back a payload containing the created bar, barX, as well as further actions that can be applied within the context of barX. When the client then requests barX by invoking the provided URL from the get-bar[X] operation, it receives back a payload containing barX, along with the other possible further activities within this context.

This interaction between the client and server can continue in the same way as just described as long as the server provides functionality metadata that can be discovered by the client.

A key benefit of using HATEOAS is that the client application does not need to have any prior knowledge of URLs of resources on the server. Instead, it only knows of the particular action names. Figure 9-2 shows how HATEOAS can facilitate the flow in an example application.

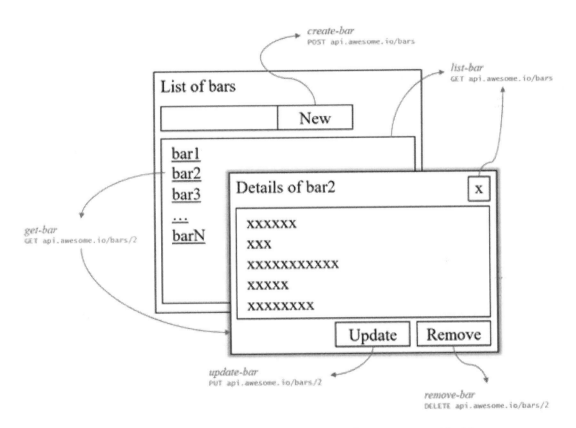

Figure 9-2. *An example application making use of actions provided by a HATEOAS-enabled server*

Implementing HATEOAS in ASP.NET Core is straightforward. Resources from the API are wrapped in an object with an additional property that contains links to other resources relevant to the particular support. Each link item inside the collection has all the information needed to successfully link to the other resource in question, like the relation key, the URL of the endpoint, and the HTTP method for the request.

Let's take an example API that provides information about people, where the person resource type may be represented by the following data transfer object:

```
public class PersonDto
{
    public int Id { get; set; }
    public string Name { get; set; }
    public string Email { get; set; }
}
```

The People API is represented in the PeopleController, which contains the endpoints to retrieve a collection of persons or a single person, create a new person, or update and remove a person:

```
[Route("api/[controller]")]
public class PeopleController : Controller
{
    //...

    [HttpGet(Name = "get-people")]
    public IActionResult Get()
    {
        //...

        return Ok(people);
    }

    [HttpGet("{id}", Name = "get-person")]
    public IActionResult Get(int id)
    {
        //...

        return Ok(person);
    }

    [HttpPost(Name = "create-person")]
    public IActionResult Post([FromBody]PersonDto person)
    {
        //...
```

```
        return Created(...);
    }

    [HttpPut("{id}", Name = "update-person")]
    public IActionResult Put(int id, [FromBody]PersonDto person)
    {
        //...

        return Ok();
    }

    [HttpDelete("{id}", Name = "delete-person")]
    public IActionResult Delete(int id)
    {
        //...

        return Ok();
    }
}
```

As a first step in converting the preceding code to a HATEOAS-enabled API, we need to create an object for holding the links, as well as two wrapper classes for wrapping a single resource and wrapping a collection of resources:

```
public class Link
{
    public Link(string rel, string href, string method)
    {
        this.Rel = rel;
        this.Href = href;
        this.Method = method;
    }

    public string Href { get; set; }
    public string Rel { get; set; }
    public string Method { get; set; }
}
```

```
public abstract class Resource
{
    [JsonProperty("_links", Order = -2)]
    public List<Link> Links { get; } = new List<Link>();
}

public class ResourceList<T>
{
    public ResourceList(List<T> items)
    {
        this.Items = items;
    }

    public List<T> Items { get; }
    [JsonProperty("_links", Order = -2)]
    public List<Link> Links { get; } = new List<Link>();
}
```

In the preceding code, the Link class contains three properties, Rel, Url, and Method, which are used for holding the link relation key, the URL of an endpoint, and the HTTP method to be used for the request, respectively. Furthermore, the Resource and ResourceList classes each contain a property of type List<Link> for holding multiple links per resource. ResourceList also contains a property called Items of type List<T>, where T represents the type of the resource.

Inside the Resource and ResourceList<T> classes, the JsonProperty attribute is used to serialize the particular property to JSON. For the Links property, an Order of -2 is defined to ensure that it renders first.

We can now extend the existing PersonDto class to be a resource, allowing the class to inherit the properties of a HATEOAS resource:

```
public class PersonDto: Resource
{
    //...
}
```

To return a collection of persons, we need to wrap the collection in an instance of
ResourceList<PersonDto>:

```
[HttpGet(Name = "get-people")]
public IActionResult Get()
{
    //...

    var result = new ResourceList<PersonDto>(people);
    return Ok(result);
}
```

Now, when we run the application and make a request to the get-people endpoint, we
will get a response with a collection of persons, but also with an empty collection of links:

```
{
  "_links": [],
  "items": [
    {
      "_links": [],
      "id": 1,
      "name": "Fanie",
      "email": "fanie@reynders.co"
    },
    {
      "_links": [],
      "id": 2,
      "name": "Maarten",
      "email": "maarten@example.com"
    },
    {
      "_links": [],
      "id": 2,
      "name": "Marcel",
      "email": "marcel@example.com"
    }
  ]
}
```

The final thing to do is to add the relevant links for each resource in the response. To keep things simple, we will only add the resource links for the get-people and get-person endpoints:

```
[HttpGet(Name = "get-people")]
public IActionResult Get()
{
    //...

    var result = new ResourceList<PersonDto>(people);

    result.Items.ForEach(p =>
    {
        p.Links.Add(new Link("self", Url.Link("get-people", new { id = p.Id
        }), "GET"));
        p.Links.Add(new Link("get-person", Url.Link("get-person", new { id
        = p.Id }), "GET"));
    });

    result.Links.Add(new Link("create-person", Url.Link("create-person",
    null), "POST"));

    return Ok(result);
}

[HttpGet("{id}", Name = "get-person")]
public IActionResult Get(int id)
{
    //...

    person.Links.Add(new Link("self", Url.Link("get-person", new { id }),
    "GET"));
    person.Links.Add(new Link("update-person", Url.Link("update-person",
    new { id }), "UPDATE"));
    person.Links.Add(new Link("delete-person", Url.Link("delete-person",
    new { id }), "DELETE"));

    return Ok(person);
}
```

> **Note**   It is considered a best practice to include a link to the resource itself with the relation key as self.

Now, when we invoke one of the endpoints, the response will contain the links we've added to the particular resource response. Here's an example response of the get-people endpoint:

```
{
  "_links": [
    {
      "href": "http://localhost:49185/api/People",
      "rel": "create-person",
      "method": "POST"
    }
  ],
  "items": [
    {
      "_links": [
        {
          "href": "http://localhost:49185/api/People/1",
          "rel": "self",
          "method": "GET"
        },
        {
          "href": "http://localhost:49185/api/People/1",
          "rel": "update-person",
          "method": "UPDATE"
        },
        {
          "href": "http://localhost:49185/api/People/1",
          "rel": "delete-person",
          "method": "DELETE"
        }
      ],
```

```
      "id": 1,
      "name": "Fanie",
      "email": "fanie@reynders.co"
    },
    //...
  ]
}
```

When we select the first resource from the preceding list and execute the get-person relation from the links provided, we will get the following response, which contains further links for any additional functionality within scope:

```
{
  "_links": [
    {
      "href": "http://localhost:49185/api/People/1",
      "rel": "update-person",
      "method": "UPDATE"
    },
    {
      "href": "http://localhost:49185/api/People/1",
      "rel": "delete-person",
      "method": "DELETE"
    }
  ],
  "id": 1,
  "name": "fanie",
  "email": "fanie@reynders.co"
}
```

Note The preceding examples are tailored to show the basics of implementing a HATEOAS-based API using ASP.NET Core MVC. There are other third-party frameworks out there that can be used to implement HATEOAS APIs in ASP.NET Core. One of them is my little project, called *aspnetcore-hateoas*, for which you can find the GitHub repository here: https://github.com/faniereynders/ aspnetcore-hateoas.

Versioning

When it comes down to the hardcore REST practices, there are endless different religious debates by so-called REST evangelists, and one of the topics in these discussions is *versioning*. Although Roy Fielding strongly recommended *against* versioning RESTful APIs, the reality is that sometimes we have no choice. In specific scenarios, being practical is more beneficial to the theory.

So, why would we want to version our APIs anyway? Well, the most straightforward answer, in my opinion, is that we don't live in a perfect world and we are always faced with possible legacy decisions that cannot be reversed, especially in the context of public APIs.

We shouldn't go wild and version everything, because improper versioning can quickly get out of control when it comes to custom implementations. We should implement versioning with caution and should always strive to have our APIs be backward compatible at all times.

All APIs must support explicit versioning to be compliant with the *REST API Guidelines* outlined by Microsoft because clients need to be dependent on services that are stable over time, mainly when more features are added that could cause breaking changes.

APIs are usually versioned using the `Major.Minor` versioning scheme, but can be optionally used in conjunction with group versioning, which uses a *date formatting scheme*, as YYY-MM-DD. Under the hood, group versioning maps to the appropriate `Major.Minor` version.

Versions of APIs can be located in four places, namely in the URL as a query string parameter, in the URL as a URL path segment, like a key in the header of a request, or defined as part of a specific media type. Here are some examples of the different options for versioning APIs:

- Version as a query string parameter in the URL:

  `https://api.awesome.io/people?api-version=1.0`

- Version as a URL segment in the URL:

  `https://api.awesome.io/v1.0/people`

- Version as a key in the header of the request:

```
GET /people HTTP/1.1
Host: api.awesome.io
api-version: 1.0
```

- Version as part of a media type:

```
GET /people HTTP/1.1
Host: api.awesome.io
Accept: application/json;v=1.0
```

To add versioning to our APIs in ASP.NET Core MVC, we can make use of the `Microsoft.AspNetCore.Mvc.Versioning` package that we will find under the default NuGet feed.

Tip   In Visual Studio, NuGet packages can be added using the user interface by right-clicking on the project and selecting *Manage NuGet Packages*, or by executing the `Install-Package` command in the *Package Manager Console*.

To install the `Microsoft.AspNetCore.Mvc.Versioning` package using the Package Manager Console, we can execute the following command:

```
Install-Package Microsoft.AspNetCore.Mvc.Versioning
```

We can also install this package via the .NET CLI by executing the following command in Command Prompt or Bash:

```
$ dotnet add package Microsoft.AspNetCore.Mvc.Versioning
```

After the package is installed, we add the versioning functionality to the services collection by calling the provided `AddApiVersioning` extension method:

```
public void ConfigureServices(IServiceCollection services )
{
    services.AddMvc();
    services.AddApiVersioning();

    //...
}
```

The preceding code will register the versioning middleware and assume that the version of the application is version 1.0. The following is a controller class AwesomeController that contains only one endpoint that returns the current version of the application:

```
namespace AwesomeApi.Controllers
{
    [Route("api/awesome")]
    public class AwesomeController : Controller
    {
        public IActionResult Get() => Ok("Version 1");
    }
}
```

When we run the application and try to invoke the People API by executing a request to /api/people, we notice the following response:

```
HTTP/1.1 400 Bad Request
Content-Type: application/json; charset=utf-8

...

{
    "Error": {
        "Code": "ApiVersionUnspecified",
        "Message": "An API version is required, but was not specified."
    }
}
```

The Bad Request response that is returned explains that an API version is required, which was not specified. Executing the same request again, but this time appending the version number as a query parameter ?api-version=1.0, will return a successful response with the expected OK response:

```
HTTP/1.1 200 OK
Content-Type: text/plain; charset=utf-8

...

Version 1
```

> **Note**   The version specified must either match the `Major.Minor` schema or group version, defined in a date format YYYY-MM-DD. When working with the `Major.Minor` format, we can either specify the whole number, for example, `api-version=1.0`, or part thereof, like `api-version=1`.

Let's now extend the application by adding new functionality. In version 2.0, we want the /api/awesome endpoint to return the current version as well as the connection identifier, as follows:

```
namespace AwesomeApi.Controllers
{
    [ApiVersion("1.0")]
    [Route("api/awesome")]
    public class AwesomeV1Controller : Controller
    {
        public IActionResult Get() => Ok("Version 1");
    }

    [ApiVersion("2.0")]
    [Route("api/awesome")]
    public class AwesomeV2Controller : Controller
    {
        public IActionResult Get() => Ok($"Version 2 - {Request.
        HttpContext.Connection.Id}");
    }
}
```

One thing that is important in the changes made to the preceding code is that we had to set the previous version as 1.0 explicitly. Otherwise, it will be used as the latest version if no version is specified in the request. Because class names need to be unique, we also had to rename the controllers accordingly.

Personally, I prefer not mixing version numbers with class or method names as it decreases the readability of the code, and I firmly believe that namespaces are the perfect place for different versions instead. After refactoring the preceding code, we end up with the following:

```
namespace AwesomeApi.Controllers.V1
{
    [ApiVersion("1.0")]
    [Route("api/awesome")]
    public class AwesomeController : Controller
    {
        public IActionResult Get() => Ok("Version 1");
    }
}
```

```
namespace AwesomeApi.Controllers.V2
{
    [ApiVersion("2.0")]
    [Route("api/awesome")]
    public class AwesomeController : Controller
    {
        public IActionResult Get() => Ok($"Version 2 - {Request.
        HttpContext.Connection.Id}" );
    }
}
```

Now, after running the application and invoking the /api/awesome?version=2.0 endpoint, we notice the following response:

```
HTTP/1.1 200 OK
Content-Type: text/plain; charset=utf-8

...

Version 2 - OHLA68RORHP5A
```

The preceding example code showed how we could implement versioning that is specified in the URL as a query parameter. In the next example, we will change the application to require the version number as a URL segment instead:

```
namespace AwesomeApi.Controllers.V1
{
    [ApiVersion("1.0")]
    [Route("api/v{version:apiVersion}/awesome")]
```

```
    public class AwesomeController : Controller
    {
        public IActionResult Get() => Ok("Version 1");
    }
}

namespace AwesomeApi.Controllers.V2
{
    [ApiVersion("2.0")]
    [Route("api/v{version:apiVersion}/awesome")]
    public class AwesomeController : Controller
    {
        public IActionResult Get() => Ok($"Version 2 - {Request.
        HttpContext.Connection.Id}");
    }
}
```

As we can see, it is simply mapping the version variable in the URL to the apiVersion.

It is very common to specify the version in the request header, as this keeps the URLs clean and uncluttered with version information. To enable request-header versioning, we need to set the ApiVersionReader option in the ConfigureServices method of the Startup class:

```
public void ConfigureServices(IServiceCollection services)
{
    //...

    services.AddApiVersioning(options =>
    {
        options.ApiVersionReader = new HeaderApiVersionReader
        ("x-api-version");
    });
}
```

The preceding code will allow us to specify the desired version of the application by setting the x-api-version header value in the request. In this example, we explicitly named the header value x-api-version, but it can be a string value. If no name is specified, it defaults to the api-version header key.

Note   Setting the version source as the header will override any version specified in the query string.

If there is a need to support version numbers specified in both the query string and the header, although not compliant with the Microsoft REST Guidelines, we can combine IApiVersionReader implementations to accommodate the need:

```
public void ConfigureServices(IServiceCollection services)
{
    //...

    services.AddApiVersioning(options =>
    {
        options.ApiVersionReader = ApiVersionReader.Combine(
            new QueryStringApiVersionReader(),
            new HeaderApiVersionReader()
            {
                HeaderNames = { "api-version" }
            });
    });
}
```

To have the version be specified as part of the content type in the header, we can make use of the MediaTypeApiVersionReader implementation:

```
public void ConfigureServices(IServiceCollection services)
{
    //...

    services.AddApiVersioning(options =>
    {
        options.ApiVersionReader = new MediaTypeApiVersionReader();
    });
}
```

The preceding configuration will allow us to specify the version as part of the content type in the Accept header; for example, Accept: application/json;v=2, which will use version number 2. We can customize the v variable by passing a custom version variable name in the constructor of the MediaTypeApiVersionReader class.

The examples showed so far were based on different versions per controller, but what if we wanted to extend the functionality of a given API to be based on action level? For example, let's say we have a Names API that, in version one, only outputs a name when requested, but in version two allows the name to be updated as well.

To implement versioning on an action level, we need to make use of the [MapToApiVersion] attribute:

```
[ApiVersion("1.0")]
[ApiVersion("2.0")]
[Route("api/[controller]")]
public class NamesController : Controller
{
    [MapToApiVersion("1.0")]
    public IActionResult Get()
    {
        //...
    }

    [MapToApiVersion("2.0")]
    public IActionResult Put(string name)
    {
        //...
    }
}
```

We can further customize how the versioning mechanism behaves by setting the desired options in the ConfigureServices method inside the Startup class. The following code highlights a few options:

```
public void ConfigureServices(IServiceCollection services)
{
    //...
```

```
services.AddApiVersioning(options =>
{
    options.DefaultApiVersion = new ApiVersion(1,0);
    options.AssumeDefaultVersionWhenUnspecified = true;
    options.ReportApiVersions = true;
});
}
```

In the preceding example, we can specify a default version either by passing the major and minor version numbers or by specifying a group version value. The default version can be assumed if no version is specified by setting the AssumeDefaultVersionWhenUnspecified option. The ReportApiVersions option allows the response to contain an additional api-supported-versions header detailing the versions that are supported for the particular request.

Note   To read more on the versioning functionality provided in this section, please visit the *aspnet-api-versioning* GitHub repository here: `https://github.com/ Microsoft/aspnet-api-versioning`.

Swagger

If you haven't heard about Swagger before, this section will quickly bring you up to speed in what it is and how we can leverage parts of it in ASP.NET Core to add a little something extra to our APIs.

Swagger is an open source framework that helps us design, build, document, and consume RESTful services, and it provides many different tools for developing, interacting with, and documenting APIs. According to their website at `https://swagger.io`, it is the world's most popular API tooling and has been adopted by the community for enabling development across the entire API lifecycle. It is part of the *OpenAPI Specification* (OAS).

Note   This section will not cover all the functionality of Swagger and is limited to include specific parts related to ASP.NET Core.

From the many features that Swagger provides, one of the most commonly used is probably the specification itself, which provides a machine-readable representation of a RESTful API for interactive documentation, client SDK code generation, and API discovery.

Going back to one of the first examples in this chapter, we will build on top of the initial People API.

Swagger can help us to generate API documentation and interactive help pages for our APIs in ASP.NET Core by using the Swashbuckle.AspNetCore NuGet package, which can be installed from within Visual Studio or just by running a simple command from the CLI:

```
$ dotnet add package Swashbuckle.AspNetCore
```

To register the Swagger middleware, we need to call the AddSwaggerGen extension method in the ConfigureServices of the Startup class:

```
public void ConfigureServices(IServiceCollection services)
{
    services.AddMvc();

    services.AddSwaggerGen(c =>
    {
        c.SwaggerDoc("v1", new Info { Title = "Awesome API", Version = "v1" });
    });
}
```

The preceding code will create an API documentation generator and call it *"v1"*. The next step is to configure the application to use the Swagger features we need:

```
public void Configure(IApplicationBuilder app, IHostingEnvironment env)
{
    app.UseSwagger();
    app.UseSwaggerUI(c =>
    {
        c.SwaggerEndpoint("/swagger/v1/swagger.json", "My API V1");
    });

    app.UseMvc();
}
```

In the preceding code, the UseSwagger function will expose an endpoint that serves a machine-readable representation of the API that is the metadata of the API in JSON format. The following example is a snippet of the response when executing the Swagger endpoint:

```
{
  "swagger": "2.0",
  "info": {
    "version": "v1",
    "title": "Awesome API"
  },
  "basePath": "/",
  "paths": {
    "/api/People": {
      "get": //...
      "post": //...
    "/api/People/{id}": {
      "get": //...
      "put": //...
      "delete": //...
    }
  },
  "definitions": {
    "PersonDto": //...
  },
  "securityDefinitions": {}
}
```

The UseSwaggerUI function exposes a user interface that uses the Swagger endpoint, which can be used as interactive documentation of our API. Figure 9-3 shows a glimpse of navigating to the /swagger endpoint using a browser.

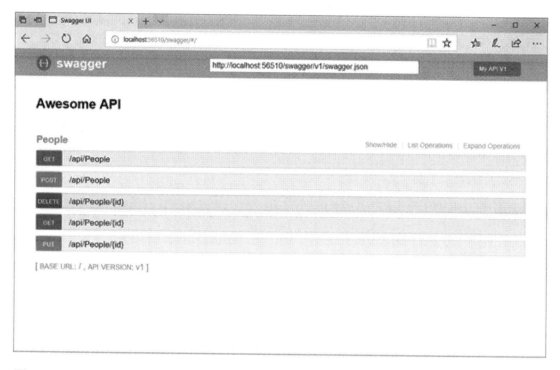

Figure 9-3. *The Swagger page for a sample API*

The actions that are displayed are interactive. Figure 9-4 shows how the screen changes when we click on one of the listed actions, like POST /api/People, for example.

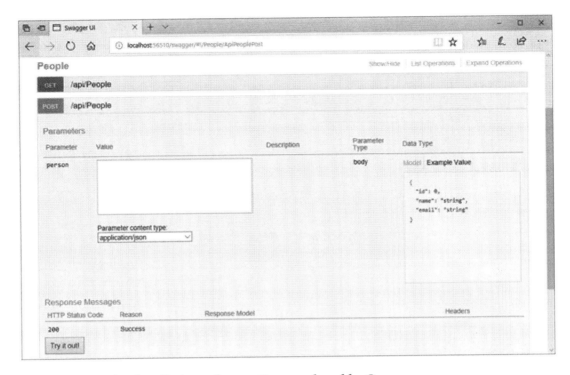

Figure 9-4. *The detail view of an action rendered by Swagger*

As we can see, it prompts us for the required parameters to try out the API while describing the API helpfully and interactively.

> **Note** To read more on the customization and extensibility of Swagger in ASP.NET Core, please visit the official documentation at `https://docs.microsoft.com/en-us/aspnet/core/tutorials/web-api-help-pages-using-swagger`.

GraphQL

Let's now shift our focus to a whole different topic that will add bells and whistles to our APIs. GraphQL is a query language for APIs that was developed by Facebook in 2012 before it became public in 2015, and it includes a runtime for executing requested queries on your existing data.

The power of GraphQL is that it allows clients to specify precisely what they need, and nothing more, which makes it easier to use as APIs evolve. Let's take a look at a simple example GraphQL query:

```
{
  person {
    name
    email
  }
}
```

The preceding GraphQL query will return the following response:

```
{
  "data": {
    "person": {
      "name": "Fanie",
      "email": "fanie@reynders.co"
    }
  }
}
```

As we see in the preceding code, the response is almost identical to the request. If we want further information on a person, let's say their friends, we simply add the properties we need:

```
{
  person {
    name
    email
    friends {
      name
    }
  }
}
```

After this GraphQL query processes, it will return a result like the following:

```
{
  "data": {
    "person": {
      "name": "Fanie",
      "email": "fanie@reynders.co",
      "friends": [
        {
          "name": "Gerald"
        },
        {
          "name": "Joe"
        },
        {
          "name": "Albert"
        }
      ]
    }
  }
}
```

> **Note**   The aim of this section is only to show how one can integrate GraphQL within an ASP.NET Core application. To learn more about GraphQL, please visit `http://graphql.org`.

The GraphQL query is sent to a particular GraphQL endpoint, which executes the query and returns the result as a GraphQL object result. One of the great things about GraphQL is that it can coexist with REST, meaning that it is merely an extension of the current system, not a replacement. You can still expose your usual RESTful endpoints and have the GraphQL endpoint live in harmony with them. GraphQL is not a replacement for REST per se, but more of an alternative extension.

Let's go ahead and implement a GraphQL endpoint in our application. We start off with our domain model, which includes a Person class with basic properties, including Friends, which is a collection of type Person[]:

```
public class Person
{
    public int Id { get; set; }
    public string Name { get; set; }
    public string Email { get; set; }
    public Person[] Friends { get; set; } = new Person[] { };
}
```

To access people information, we have an IPeopleRepository for exposing queries to get all people and those to get a specific person by Id:

```
public interface IPersonRepository
{
    IEnumerable<Person> GetAll();
    Person GetOne(int id);
}
```

Before we go any further, we need to add a NuGet package to our project, called GraphQL:

```
dotnet add package GraphQL
```

Now we can start to implement the GraphQL endpoint by creating a middleware class called AwesomeGraphQLMiddleware:

```
public class AwesomeGraphQLMiddleware
{
    private readonly RequestDelegate _next;
    private readonly IPersonRepository _personRepository;

    public AwesomeGraphQLMiddleware(RequestDelegate next, IPersonRepository
    personRepository)
    {
        _next = next;
        _personRepository = personRepository;
    }
```

```csharp
public async Task Invoke(HttpContext httpContext)
{
    if (httpContext.Request.Path.StartsWithSegments("/graphql"))
    {
        using (var stream = new StreamReader(httpContext.Request.Body))
        {
            var query = await stream.ReadToEndAsync();
            if (!String.IsNullOrWhiteSpace(query))
            {
                var schema = new Schema { Query = new PersonQuery
                (_personRepository) };

                var result = await new DocumentExecuter()
                    .ExecuteAsync(options =>
                    {
                        options.Schema = schema;
                        options.Query = query;
                    });
                await WriteResult(httpContext, result);
            }
        }
    }
    else
    {
        await _next(httpContext);
    }
}

private async Task WriteResult(HttpContext httpContext, ExecutionResult result)
{
    var json = new DocumentWriter(indent: true).Write(result);

    httpContext.Response.StatusCode = 200;
    httpContext.Response.ContentType = "application/json";
    await httpContext.Response.WriteAsync(json);
}
}
```

When invoked, it verifies that the request path is /graphql and then attempts to read the body of the request using a StreamReader. A Schema object is then constructed, with the Query property set as an instance of a PersonQuery, which takes in an instance of an IPersonRepository.

After a new DocumentExecuter is created that executes the query against the provided schema, the result is written to the response as JSON by calling the WriteResult function.

The PersonQuery contains the implementation details for GraphQL, and herein we map all the fields for a given query to the appropriate call on the repository:

```
public class PersonQuery : ObjectGraphType
{
    public PersonQuery(IPersonRepository personRepository)
    {
        Field<PersonType>("person",
            arguments: new QueryArguments(
                new QueryArgument<IntGraphType>() { Name = "id" }),
            resolve: context =>
            {
                var id = context.GetArgument<int>("id");
                return personRepository.GetOne(id);
            });

        Field<ListGraphType<PersonType>>("people",
            resolve: context =>
            {
                return personRepository.GetAll();
            });
    }
}
```

Drilling down a bit further, the PersonType is a GraphQL-specific type and contains explicitly defined fields that are mapped to the Person domain object:

```
public class PersonType : ObjectGraphType<Person>
{
```

```
    public PersonType()
    {
        Field(x => x.Id);
        Field(x => x.Name);
        Field(x => x.Email);
        Field<ListGraphType<PersonType>>("friends");
    }
}
```

The last thing to do is to wire up the dependencies and register the GraphQLMiddleware we've just created:

```
public void ConfigureServices(IServiceCollection services)
{
    //...

    services.AddSingleton<IPersonRepository, PersonRepository>();
}
public void Configure(IApplicationBuilder app)
{
    app.UseMiddleware<AwesomeGraphQLMiddleware>();

    //...
}
```

We are now finally ready to test out this beast. After a quick compile, we run the application and post the following GraphQL query to the /graphql endpoint:

```
{
  person(id:1) {
    name
    friends {
      name
        email
      }
  }
}
```

Figure 9-5 shows the output when executing this GraphQL query using a client like Postman.

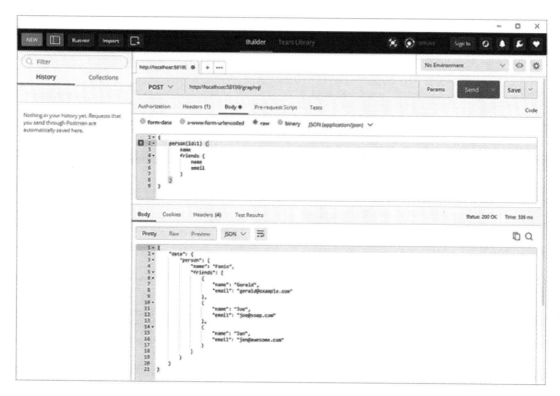

Figure 9-5. *Output from a GraphQL query in ASP.NET Core*

Wrapping Up

We've come to the end of yet another chapter. I hope that you enjoyed reading this chapter as much as I enjoyed writing it. This chapter was all about adding that extra bling to our APIs to make them stand out and shine.

We started off by exploring the concept of HATEOAS, including how it relates to REST and how it can help us to implement a stateless API. After that, we delved into versioning and explored a few ways of achieving versioning within our ASP.NET Core applications. We covered the use of Swagger in our applications and how it can contribute to automatic interactive documentation generation for our APIs. We ended this chapter with a bang, in my opinion, by diving head first into implementing a GraphQL endpoint that will allow clients to query precisely what they need from our service.

In the next chapter, we will look at testing web APIs and what ASP.NET Core has to offer to improve the quality of our code.

CHAPTER 10

Testing & Debugging

It is time to shift our focus to another important part of API design, which is the testing and debugging of the source code. This chapter will briefly share some interesting points on why testing is essential, as well as dive into the implementation details for creating unit and integration tests. Also included in this chapter will be complete instructions on how to debug the source code of compiled external libraries by using their symbols loaded from the Internet.

Why Is Testing Important?

In recent years, software testing has become an integral part of product *quality assurance* (QA). We all do some level of testing of our code before deploying it to a production environment, be it a simple little quick-and-dirty exploratory testing or full-blown automated testing that covers nearly 104 percent of the code.

One can imagine what would happen if car companies just designed, built, and released their vehicles without first doing some form of testing. Software is no different. Just like in the case of cars, users rely on working software to do their daily tasks.

In the context of software development, testing is the process of verifying if a particular software component satisfies a specific functional requirement and a way to gain insight into the test-result metrics to ensure that the quality of the software is on a certain level.

To accelerate development turnaround times and to do testing consistently, we make use of testing tools and frameworks that allow us to perform automated testing tasks against structured scenarios. Test automation reduces the risk of human error because humans suck at routine jobs, but machines thrive at them.

185

© Fanie Reynders 2018
F. Reynders, *Modern API Design with ASP.NET Core 2*, https://doi.org/10.1007/978-1-4842-3519-5_10

Software testing methods, such as unit testing and integration testing, are used within testing frameworks to facilitate the verification process for a specific scenario. As software development evolves, more sophisticated development processes arise, like *test-driven development* (TDD) and *behavior-driven development* (BDD).

TDD is a process of developing software in the repetition of short iterations. Functional requirements are transformed into specific test cases that should fail upon initial execution. Just enough software is written to make a particular test case pass, then, if need be, the software is refactored to improve code quality. As a result of refactoring, some test cases might again fail, and then the whole process starts all over by either changing the test case or changing the software code.

BDD is derived from TDD and combines the techniques and principles of TDD with the ideas of *object-oriented design* (OOD) and *domain-driven design* (DDD). The structure of test cases in BDD leans toward a *user story* that contains a title, a short narrative detailing *who, what,* and *why,* as well as *acceptance criteria* to validate if the requirement is satisfied.

One of the main reasons why testing is necessary is not just the metrics it produces, but also the quality it ensures during the software development process. Test cases align with the code coverage of unit and integration tests to provide useful insights, whether tests cover all or only some of the scenarios.

Unit Testing

In this section, we will be exploring the implementation of unit tests using some of the tools made available by Microsoft and the community. We will be building a solution from scratch to learn the basics of creating unit tests in .NET Core.

Open your favorite shell program, like PowerShell, and create a new folder in a location of your choice called *awesometests* by running `mkdir .\awesometests`. This folder will hold the solution for the examples. Move into that folder by executing `cd .\awesometests`.

Using the .NET Core CLI, run the following commands to create a new solution in the directory created in the previous step and to add a *class library* called AwesomeService to the solution; this library will contain some business logic to test later:

```
$ dotnet new sln
$ dotnet new classlib -n AwesomeService
$ dotnet sln add .\AwesomeService\AwesomeService.csproj
```

With your favorite code editor, open the current directory. If you're using Visual Studio Code, you can simply run code . to open Visual Studio Code in the current directory.

Under the AwesomeService directory, remove the class file called Class1.cs, which was automatically created by default, and create a new file called Calculators.cs that contains the following code:

```
using System;

namespace AwesomeService
{
    public interface ICalculator
    {
        int Add(int nr1, int nr2);
    }

    public class AwesomeCalculator : ICalculator
    {
        public int Add(int nr1, int nr2)
        {
            throw new NotImplementedException();
        }
    }
}
```

Back in the shell window, add a new *XUnit* project called AwesomeService.Tests to the solution and add a project reference to AwesomeService.csproj by executing the following CLI commands:

```
$ dotnet new xunit -n AwesomeService.Tests
$ dotnet sln add .\AwesomeService.Tests\AwesomeService.Tests.csproj
$ cd .\AwesomeService.Tests
$ dotnet add reference ..\AwesomeService\AwesomeService.csproj
```

Now we are ready to start writing some unit tests. To follow the principles of TDD, we write a failing test first, then implement just enough code to make the test pass, then repeat the whole process. Toggle back to the code editor and remove the file UnitTest1.cs, which was automatically created by default, and then add a new class called AwesomeCalculatorTest.cs containing the following code:

```
using System;
using Xunit;

namespace AwesomeService.Tests
{
    public class AwesomeCalculator_Add_Should
    {
        [Fact]
        public void Return_2_Given_Value_Of_1_And_1()
        {
            ICalculator calculator = new AwesomeCalculator();
            var result = calculator.Add(1,1);
            Assert.Equal(2, result);
        }
    }
}
```

In the preceding code, the [Fact] attribute indicates that the method attached to it is a test. In the test, we create a new instance of AwesomeCalculator as an ICalculator and then call the Add method on it; we expect the result to be 2.

From the shell window, switch to the .\AwesomeService.Tests directory and run the following command to run the test:

```
$ dotnet test
```

After running the preceding test command, we will see the following output on the console detailing the results of the test:

```
Starting test execution, please wait...
[xUnit.net 00:00:00.5405563]    Discovering: AwesomeService.Tests
[xUnit.net 00:00:00.6283882]    Discovered:  AwesomeService.Tests
[xUnit.net 00:00:00.6362569]    Starting:    AwesomeService.Tests
[xUnit.net 00:00:00.8426874]    AwesomeService.Tests.AwesomeCalculator_Add_
                                Should.Return_2_Given_Value_Of_1_And_1 [FAIL]
[xUnit.net 00:00:00.8448852]        System.NotImplementedException : The
                                    method or operation is not implemented.
...
```

Total tests: 1. Passed: 0. Failed: 1. Skipped: 0.
Test Run Failed.

The output indicates that one test was found and run, resulting as *failed* because a NotImplementedException was thrown.

Now that we have a failing test, let's go back to the AwesomeCalculator class and implement the Add method:

```
public int Add(int nr1, int nr2)
{
    return nr1 + nr2;
}
```

After executing the dotnet test command again at the terminal window, it passes:

```
...
```

Total tests: 1. Passed: 1. Failed: 0. Skipped: 0.
Test Run Successful.

Following an iteration, let's introduce a change in business logic by adding a third number to be included in the addition operation. We do this by changing the Add method in the ICalculator interface to include a third variable called nr3, and we also introduce this variable to implement the interface in the AwesomeCalculator class accordingly:

```
public interface ICalculator
{
    int Add(int nr1, int nr2, int nr3);
}

public class AwesomeCalculator : ICalculator
{
    public int Add(int nr1, int nr2, int nr3)
    {
        return nr1 + nr2;
    }
}
```

Now we need to change our test to also take the third number into account in its verification process:

```
[Fact]
public void Return_4_Given_Value_Of_1_And_1_And_2()
{
    ICalculator calculator = new AwesomeCalculator();
    var result = calculator.Add(1,1,2);
    Assert.Equal(4, result);
}
```

Running the test again, we will notice that it fails again:

```
...
AwesomeService.Tests.AwesomeCalculator_Add_Should.Return_4_Given_Value_
Of_1_And_1_And_2 [FAIL]
[xUnit.net 00:00:01.2298122]        Assert.Equal() Failure
[xUnit.net 00:00:01.2299612]        Expected: 4
[xUnit.net 00:00:01.2300141]        Actual:   2
...

Total tests: 1. Passed: 0. Failed: 1. Skipped: 0.
Test Run Failed.
```

Going back to the AwesomeCalculator class, let's fix the bug by also taking the third number variable into account in the addition operation:

```
public int Add(int nr1, int nr2, int nr3)
{
    return nr1 + nr2 + nr3;
}
```

After fixing the code, running the tests again will result in a passed test:

```
...
Total tests: 1. Passed: 1. Failed: 0. Skipped: 0.
Test Run Successful.
```

The unit test only covers one scenario, namely three numbers being 1, 1, and 2, respectively. We can create another test method that covers more scenarios, but it can get quite messy because the same code is tested with different parameters.

Instead of creating multiple tests that only contain different variables, we can replace the [Fact] attribute with the [Theory] and [InlineData] attributes on the test method. A [Theory] test contains many scenarios for one test method. Let's modify our test method to support many scenarios:

```
[Theory]
[InlineData(1, 2, 3)]
[InlineData(3, 2, 1)]
[InlineData(7, 7, 7)]
public void Return_Sum_Of_Values(int nr1, int nr2, int nr3)
{
    ICalculator calculator = new AwesomeCalculator();
    var actualResult = calculator.Add(nr1, nr2, nr3);
    var expectedResult = nr1 + nr2 + nr3;
    Assert.Equal(expectedResult, actualResult);
}
```

The modified test method will be seen as three tests, each covering a different scenario dictated by the data specified in the [InlineData] attribute. Executing the test runner again will result in the following output:

```
...
Total tests: 3. Passed: 3. Failed: 0. Skipped: 0.
Test Run Successful.
```

We can repeat this process over and over during the whole development process. You can imagine that repeating these steps can become quite cumbersome, but luckily there is a CLI tool that can help to automate a few things.

We can use the dotnet watch CLI tool to trigger commands whenever the source files change. It's available as a NuGet package called Microsoft.DotNet.Watcher.Tools. To install it, we just need to add the package reference to the AwesomeService.Tests project as a CLI tool. We do this by editing the AwesomeService.Tests.csproj project file and adding the following DotNetCliToolReference tag as part of an ItemGroup:

```
<ItemGroup>
    <DotNetCliToolReference Include="Microsoft.DotNet.Watcher.Tools"
    Version="2.0.0"/>
</ItemGroup>
```

After saving the project file and running dotnet restore, the dotnet watch tool is ready to be used; it has the following syntax:

dotnet watch <command>

Now, instead of just running dotnet test to execute the test runner only once, we can run the following command with dotnet watch to automatically run the test command whenever something changes:

$ dotnet watch test

While the watcher is running, whenever we make changes to the files it will automatically run all the tests that are discovered in the solution.

Dealing with Dependencies

Unit testing is focused on testing single units of work. Methods that are being tested may contain references to other dependencies, however, and if those dependencies are also encapsulated in the method during unit testing, it is not testing a single unit anymore.

When testing methods that are dependent on other components, we can make use of *mocking*, which is a process of simulating third-party behavior to isolate the unit being tested. Here's an example PersonService class that has a dependency on another IPersonRepository object:

```
public class PersonService
{
    private readonly IPersonRepository personRepository;

    public PersonService(IPersonRepository personRepository)
    {
        this.personRepository = personRepository;
    }

    public int CountLetters()
    {
        var names = personRepository.GetNames();
        var count = names.Select(n => n.Length).Sum();
        return count;
    }
}
```

The unit test responsible for testing the CountLetters method needs to provide an instance of IPersonRepository when instantiating the PersonService class, and because the PersonService is using an instance of IPersonRepository that might get data from a database, we need to simulate an instance of IPersonRepository to prevent calls to an external database.

To implement a simulated instance of IPersonRepository, we can use *Moq*, which is a mocking framework, to simulate the behavior of components during testing. To add the Moq package to the testing project from NuGet, we execute the following shell command within the folder of the test project:

```
$ dotnet add package Moq
```

We can now implement a unit test that uses Moq for creating a mocked instance of IPersonRepository:

```
[Fact]
public void Return_Count_Of_Letters()
{
    var personRepositoryMock = new Mock<IPersonRepository>();

    personRepositoryMock.Setup(p => p.GetNames())
        .Returns(new string[] { "Fanie", "Gerald", "Mike" });

    PersonService personService = new PersonService(personRepositoryMock.
    Object);

    var actualResult = personService.CountLetters();
    var expectedResult = 15;
    Assert.Equal(expectedResult, actualResult);
}
```

When creating a Moq mock, we set up certain actions to return specific expected results. In the preceding case, we created a mock that returns a fixed list of names whenever GetNames is called. Moq encapsulates the mocked object as the Object property, which is used wherever it is required.

Integration Testing

Integration testing ensures that the components of an application work as expected when they are all put together. Unlike unit testing, integration testing involves testing all implementations of individual components together, which may include infrastructure concerns.

A prime example of integration testing within the context of ASP.NET Core is controller testing. Although we can unit test action methods in a controller, the resulting test will then exclude other required components like filters, routing, and model binding, which may be crucial to the outcome. We can, of course, use a mocking framework like Moq to mock out certain parts of the components that we don't want to cover with the test.

Let's create an integration test for verifying that an endpoint of a controller returns the correct XML response. The following Startup class adds response caching, service dependencies, MVC, and the ability to format responses in XML to the application:

```
public class Startup
{
    public void ConfigureServices(IServiceCollection services)
    {
        services.AddResponseCaching();
        services.TryAddSingleton(new HttpClient());
        services.TryAddSingleton<IPeopleRepository, PeopleRepository>();
        services.AddMvc().AddXmlSerializerFormatters();
    }

    public void Configure(IApplicationBuilder app)
    {
        app.UseResponseCaching();
        app.UseMvc();
    }
}
```

Tip   In the preceding example, we use the `TryAdd...` extension method to prevent the application from overriding the service configurations, which might be explicitly overridden upon the test setup. Nothing changes during the runtime of the application, as it only adds the particular service if it hasn't been added before.

Also included in the application is a `PersonDto` class, which contains XML serialization attributes that are used for serializing the object in the correct XML format:

```
[XmlRoot("Person")
public class PersonDto
{
    [XmlAttribute]
    public int Id { get; set; }
    [XmlAttribute]
    public string Name { get; set; }
}
```

Furthermore, we have an implementation of `IPeopleRepository` that uses an `HttpClient` to get a particular customer name from a remote service and then return an instance of `PersonDto`:

```
public class PeopleRepository : IPeopleRepository
{
    private readonly HttpClient client;

    public PeopleRepository(HttpClient client)
    {
        this.client = client;
    }
    public async Task<PersonDto> GetOneAsync(int id)
    {
        var personResponse = await client.GetAsync($"https://api.awesome.io/
        customers/names/{id}");
        var personName = await personResponse.Content.ReadAsStringAsync();
```

```
        return new PersonDto
        {
            Id = id,
            Name = personName
        };
    }
}
```

Finally, we have a controller called PeopleController that contains one action method that returns the appropriate HTTP response depending on the input request:

```
[Route("api/[controller]")]
public class PeopleController : Controller
{
    private readonly IPeopleRepository peopleRepository;

    public PeopleController(IPeopleRepository peopleRepository)
    {
        this.peopleRepository = peopleRepository;
    }
    [HttpGet("{id}")]
    [ResponseCache(Duration = 30)]
    public async Task<IActionResult> Get(int? id)
    {
        if (id.HasValue)
        {
            var person = await peopleRepository.GetOneAsync(id.Value);
            if (person == null)
            {
                return NotFound();
            }
            return Ok(person);
        }
        return BadRequest();
    }
}
```

The Get action method in the preceding code receives an id parameter from the route URL string and also caches the response for thirty seconds.

There are a couple of things we need to verify as part of our integration test, namely:

- Given a valid URL route, test if it binds correctly to the input variables of the action method.

- Verify if the implementation of IPeopleRepository calls into an external service to retrieve a person's name.

- Given a valid person id, test if the HTTP status code is 200 (OK).

- Given that the Accept header is set to receive XML, test if the content type returned is indeed XML, as well as that the actual content is in XML format, also taking any XML serialization into account.

- Verify if the response contains the correct caching response headers.

The following test method is an example integration test that verifies the items just outlined:

```
public class PeopleController_Should
{
    //...

    [Fact]
    public async Task Return_Cached_Person_As_Xml_Given_Id()
    {
        //arrange
        var httpMock = CreateMockHttpClient("Fanie");
        var hostBuilder = new WebHostBuilder()
            .UseStartup<Startup>()
            .ConfigureServices(services =>
            {
                services.AddSingleton(httpMock);
            });

        var server = new TestServer(hostBuilder);
        var client = server.CreateClient();
```

```
client.DefaultRequestHeaders.Accept.Add(new
MediaTypeWithQualityHeaderValue("application/xml"));

//act
var response = await client.GetAsync("/api/people/2");
var content = await response.Content.ReadAsStringAsync();

//assert
Assert.True(response.IsSuccessStatusCode);

Assert.Equal("application/xml", response.Content.Headers.
ContentType.MediaType);
var expectedContent = "<Person xmlns:xsi=\"http://www.w3.org/2001/
XMLSchema-instance\" xmlns:xsd=\"http://www.w3.org/2001/XMLSchema\"
Id=\"2\" Name=\"Fanie\"/>";
Assert.Equal(expectedContent, content);
Assert.True(response.Headers.CacheControl.Public);
Assert.Equal(30, response.Headers.CacheControl.MaxAge.Value.
TotalSeconds);
    }
}
```

It is good practice for tests to contain clear parts indicating what the test is doing, namely *arrange*, for all test initialization logic and setup; *act*, for the actions being tested; and *assert*, for verifying the outcomes.

During the setup phase of the integration test, we create a mock instance of HttpClient that returns a string value *Fanie* for all requests because it is considered out of scope for this test. We create a new web host using the application's Startup class but then override the singleton service dependency of HttpClient with our custom mock version.

We then create a new instance of the TestServer class, which is a special implementation of IServer provided by the ASP.NET Core framework for running tests, and pass in the instance of the WebHostBuilder we created earlier.

A test client is created by calling the CreateClient method on the server, which we can use to execute requests. In the final part of the rest of the test arrangement, we add an Accept request header as application/xml.

Debugging .NET Core and ASP.NET Core Sources

Things might get a little tricky when debugging code that uses other frameworks because the source symbols that are loaded during the debugging process are specific to the application itself. Sometimes we need to jump into the code of other libraries, like .NET Core and ASP.NET Core, to understand how they work and behave. Normally packaged libraries are optimized for release and do not include the source symbols that map the compiled version to the source code. If the source code and source symbols for a particular library are available, we are able to debug and step through the code.

Visual Studio 2017 (version 15.3.5 and later) allows us to link to external library sources and step into their code while debugging our application. To do this, open the *Options dialog* in Visual Studio 2017 by clicking *Tools* and then selecting *Options*. Under the *Debugging General* section, uncheck the *Enable Just My Code* option and make sure that the *Enable Source Link* support item is selected. Figure 10-1 shows where to find these relevant options.

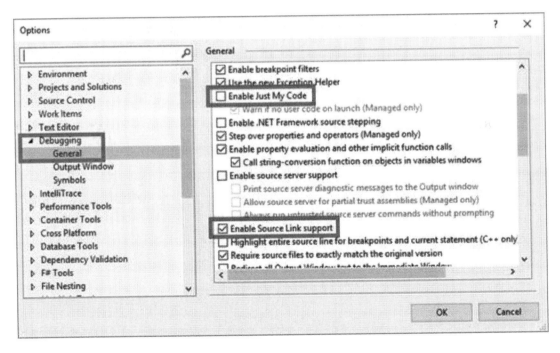

Figure 10-1. *The general debugging options*

Under the *Symbols* sub-section of *Debugging*, select *Microsoft Symbol Servers* and specify a *cache directory* for downloading cached symbols. Figure 10-2 shows how to enable the loading of symbols from Microsoft's Symbol Servers.

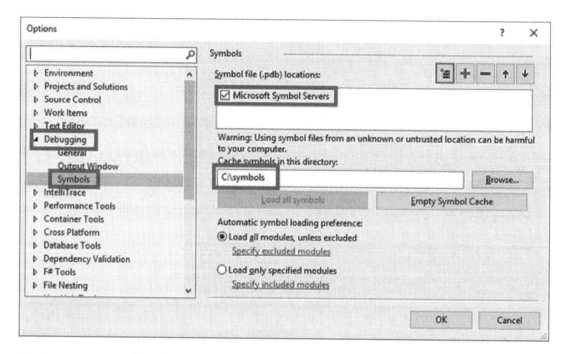

Figure 10-2. Symbol debugging options

Now we are ready to do some debugging in the source code of .NET Core and ASP. NET Core. Add a breakpoint at a given point that is calling into something from ASP.NET Core—for instance, at the return of the Ok function in the action method—and run the application to that point. Figure 10-3 shows an example breakpoint for doing this.

```
56        [HttpGet("{id}")]
          0 references | ⚡ 2 requests | 0 exceptions
57        public async Task<IActionResult> Get(int? id)
58        {
59            var person = await peopleRepository.GetOneAsync(id.Value);
60            return Ok(person);
61        }
62    }
63  }
64
```

Figure 10-3. An example breakpoint calling a function in ASP.NET Core

Tip   We can also debug code directly if it contains a bounded test by right-clicking on the test and selecting *Debug Selected Tests*.

After the debugging process has started and the breakpoint of the particular line of code is reached, we can step into the code by pressing *F11* on the keyboard. Figure 10-4 shows an example where a breakpoint has been stepped into, revealing the source code of the calling function.

```
308        /// <summary>
309        /// Creates an <see cref="OkObjectResult"/> object that produces an <see cref='
310        /// </summary>
311        /// <param name="value">The content value to format in the entity body.</param:
312        /// <returns>The created <see cref="OkObjectResult"/> for the response.</return
313        [NonAction]
314        public virtual OkObjectResult Ok(object value)
315        {
316            return new OkObjectResult(value);   ≤ 1ms elapsed
317        }
318
```

Figure 10-4. *An example line of code stepped into*

Note   It is possible that you might be prompted by a dialog to download the source code using Source Link from the internet. Just click *Download Source and Continue Debugging* to go further.

Wrapping Up

We've come to the end of yet another chapter. We learned many exciting things on the topic of testing and debugging. Looking back, we covered the importance of testing, describing the different testing techniques that are used during the development process. We delved into the implementations of unit and integration tests for ASP.NET Core applications, as well as how to mock third-party dependencies that we do not want to test. We closed this chapter by looking at an interesting way of debugging the source code of external libraries that make their source symbols available via the Internet.

Marking the end of this book, in the next chapter we will explore hosting and deployment options that are available for ASP.NET Core applications.

CHAPTER 11

Hosting & Deployment

The goal of writing any piece of software is to successfully deploy and run it in a production environment for use. Applications can run in different environments that are used for specific purposes, like developer integration testing, user acceptance testing, and, of course, production. Each environment provides an isolated host where applications can run.

The term *hosting* refers to the mechanism that provides access for the application to the end-user; hosts are typically configured on an application server in a specific environment. *Deployment* is the process of transferring an application to a host.

In this chapter, we will cover the different ways of hosting an ASP.NET Core application on different environment types, like using IIS or Windows Services on Windows, using Nginx on Linux, and using the Visual Studio Tools for Docker on Docker.

We will also explore the steps involved in publishing an ASP.NET Core application to cloud-based infrastructures, like Microsoft Azure, and how to set up a continuous integration and delivery pipeline by using Visual Studio Team Services to automatically build and deploy applications as they are checked into source control.

Hosting on Windows

When it comes to hosting ASP.NET Core applications on Windows, there are two options: on IIS or as a Windows Service. Created by Microsoft, Internet Information Services (IIS) is a web server meant for use with the Windows NT family and is available as an additional component that can be installed on the Windows operating system.

Note Although this section covers ASP.NET Core applications running on IIS, it does not include the steps for installing IIS on the compatible Windows version, and the assumption is that IIS is already installed and available.

© Fanie Reynders 2018
F. Reynders, *Modern API Design with ASP.NET Core 2*, https://doi.org/10.1007/978-1-4842-3519-5_11

Let's deploy a sample ASP.NET Core application to run under IIS. The first thing we need to do is create the destination website for the application in IIS. As shown in Figure 11-1, right-click the *Sites* node and then select *Add Website*.

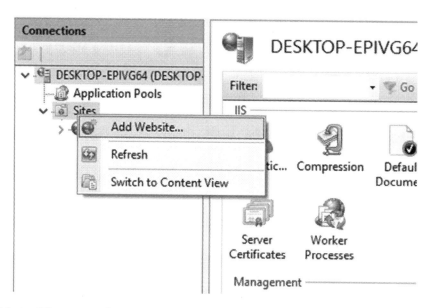

Figure 11-1. *The menu for creating a new website in IIS*

On the next window that opens, we give our site a name of *AwesomeApi* and select a physical path from which the website should be loaded. For this example, we've created a new directory under C:\inetpub\awesome, but it can be anywhere, given that IIS has sufficient access rights to the directory. In the *Binding* section, we specify the port number as *80* and bind the website to the api.awesome.io hostname. Figure 11-2 shows the configuration of the site.

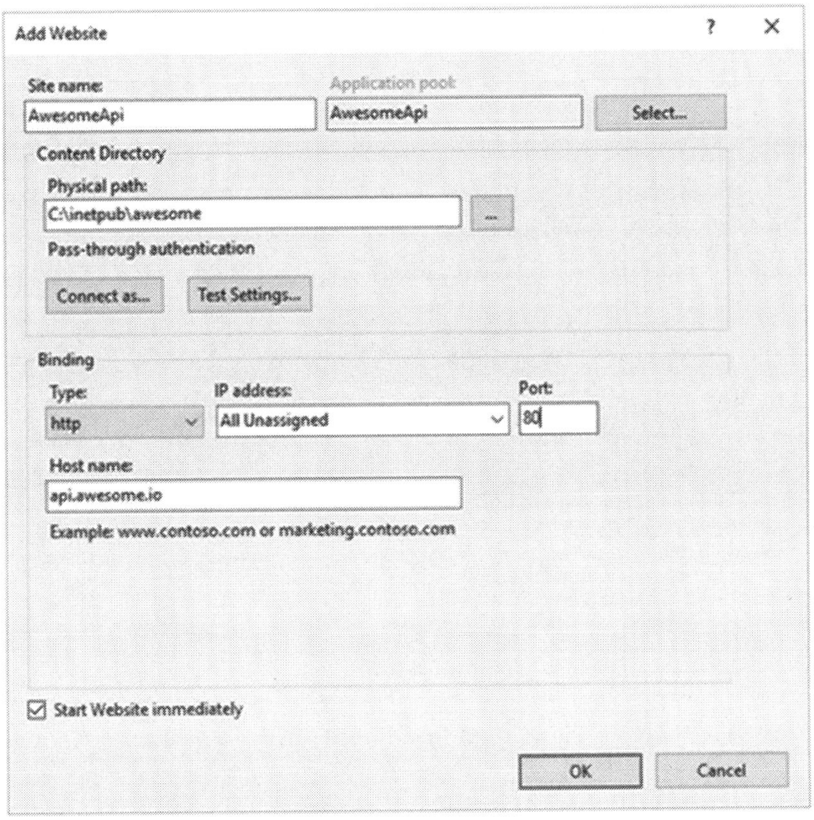

Figure 11-2. *The Add Website dialog*

Note   The domain name `api.awesome.io` is an arbitrary name only used for example purposes. In a real scenario, we would use a domain name we already own.

By default, websites created in IIS are assigned an *application pool* that is bound to the .NET Common Language Runtime (CLR) by default. Because we are going to host an ASP.NET Core application, which is independent of the .NET CLR installed on the disk, it will therefore require no managed code.

Figure 11-3 shows how to configure the application pool to not use managed code by opening the *Application Pools* node, selecting the *AwesomeApi* pool, and then setting the *.NET CLR version* to *No Managed Code*. Click *OK* to apply the changes.

205

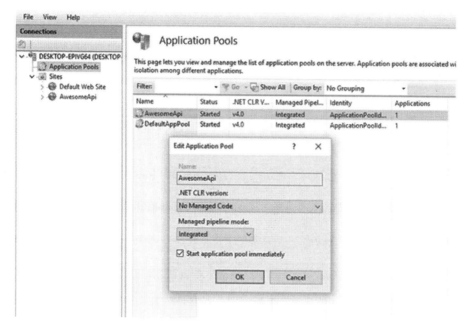

Figure 11-3. *The Edit Application Pool dialog*

Now the website is created and configured on IIS. After a quick test, requesting `http://api.awesome.io/ping` returns a `404 Not Found` response, as the directory is empty. We now need to publish our application to the *AwesomeApi* created on IIS.

In the sample application, we have an MVC controller called `PingController` that has just one endpoint for returning the result as "*Pong*":

```
[Route("[controller]")]
public class PingController : Controller
{
    public IActionResult Get() => Ok("Pong");
}
```

For simplicity, we have kept with the defaults when creating a new web host in `Program.cs` by calling the `WebHost.CreateDefaultBuilder` function. This function creates a new web host that is configured to integrate with IIS.

Open a shell window on the root of the ASP.NET Core application and run the following commands to build and package the application for deployment:

```
$ dotnet publish
```

Running this `dotnet publish` command will restore all project dependencies, compile, and package the application up for deployment. In this example, we chose to publish the application as a *framework-dependent deployment* (FDD), which means that the application will be deployed only with its third-party dependencies, and without the .NET Core framework and runtime, as we trust that .NET Core is already installed on the destination system. The FDD model is the default model for deploying .NET Core applications.

Note   The other deployment model is a *self-contained deployment* (SDC), which deploys the dependencies to .NET Core along with the application so as to run self-contained in various environments.

The last thing we need to do is copy the artifacts that were created by the `dotnet publish` command on the `.\bin\Debug\netcoreapp2.0\publish` directory to the destination directory of the *AwesomeApi*, which is in this case located at `C:\inetpub\awesome`.

Now when we request `http://api.awesome.io/ping`, we receive the proper response as *"Pong"*. How did this work? As part of the deployment, there is a `web.config` file that contains the following:

```xml
<?xml version="1.0" encoding="utf-8"?>
<configuration>
  <system.webServer>
    <handlers>
      <add name="aspNetCore" path="*" verb="*" modules="AspNetCoreModule"
      resourceType="Unspecified"/>
    </handlers>
    <aspNetCore processPath="dotnet" arguments=".\AwesomeApi.dll"
    stdoutLogEnabled="false" stdoutLogFile=".\logs\stdout"/>
  </system.webServer>
</configuration>
```

Inside the web.config file, we will find that an IIS handler called aspNetCore is added that is responsible for relaying the requests through to the application. When the website starts up, it executes dotnet .\AwesomeApi.dll, which runs our .NET Core application.

Note   As a prerequisite, the ASP.NET Core module must be installed in IIS to have requests be relayed to Kestrel. Without this module, we will get an HTTP 500.19 error when trying to invoke the application under IIS. The ASP.NET Core module is included in the Windows Server Hosting package and can be downloaded here: https://www.microsoft.com/net/download/windows.

Another way to publish an ASP.NET Core application to IIS is through a process called *web deploy*, which allows us to deploy the application right from within Visual Studio. We will explore publishing using web deploy later in this chapter.

The other option for hosting an ASP.NET Core application on Windows is doing so as a Windows Service. To make this work, the application needs to target the full .NET framework runtime. Edit the project's .csproj file and add the following code:

```
<PropertyGroup>
    <TargetFramework>net461</TargetFramework>
    <RuntimeIdentifier>win7-x86</RuntimeIdentifier>
</PropertyGroup>
```

This code indicates that the application targets the full .NET framework version 4.6.1 and should be compiled to run as a standalone application for x86-based Windows systems.

Tip   Use the ASP.NET Core Application template based on the full .NET framework to accomplish this for new projects.

To have the application run as a Windows Service, we need to make some changes to the code. To get started, we need to install the Microsoft.AspNetCore.Hosting. WindowsServices NuGet package by running the following command from the root folder of the application in a shell window:

```
$ dotnet add package Microsoft.AspNetCore.Hosting.WindowsServices
```

Installing this NuGet package will allow us to run the web host as a Windows Service. In the Program class, replace Run with RunAsService instead:

```
public static void Main(string[] args)
{
    BuildWebHost(args).RunAsService();
}
```

Next, we need to build and bundle our application for deployment by running the following command from a shell window in the root directory of the project:

```
$ dotnet publish
```

The dotnet publish command will create a self-contained application under the .\bin\Debug\net461\win7-x86\publish directory and will contain an executable called AwesomeApi.exe. We can now copy the contents of the publish directory to any directory of our choice, like C:\Services, for instance.

From the command prompt, run the following commands:

```
$ sc create AwesomeApiService binPath=c:\services\AwesomeApi.exe
$ sc start AwesomeApiService
```

The sc create command will install the application as a Windows Service and start it using sc start. When the service is running, we can test the application by invoking it on http://localhost:5000/ping, assuming port 5000 is the default port that has been set up.

Hosting on Linux

It is dead simple to deploy .NET Core applications, regardless of the operating system. Just copy the published artifacts to the destination folder and either run the application using dotnet yourapp.dll, if the .NET Core runtime is already installed on the server, or execute the application executable if the .NET Core runtime is packaged with the application as a self-contained application.

Let's use the same sample application as we did in the previous section when hosting the application in IIS and deploy it to a remote server with *Ubuntu 16.04* installed. In a shell window at the root of the project directory structure, execute the following commands to build and publish the application for the Ubuntu 16.04 distribution:

```
$ dotnet publish -r ubuntu.16.04-x64
```

The -r option in the dotnet publish command tells the .NET Core CLI to publish the application for a specific runtime as a self-contained application.

Now we can use our favorite remote copy tool, like *WinSCP* if you're developing on Windows, and copy the contents of the .\bin\Debug\netcoreapp2.0\ ubuntu.16.04-x64\publish folder to the destination folder on the server—/home/ faniereynders/awesome, for example.

To run the application, just execute the AwesomeApi executable in the /home/ faniereynders/awesome directory. If you're unable to log on to the server itself physically, you can use a tool like *PuTTY* to log in to the Linux server remotely.

Although working with Kestrel as the HTTP server is excellent, it isn't advised to have the outside world connect to Kestrel directly, because it is optimized for speed and doesn't deal with web serving as well as other servers, like IIS or Nginx, do. A reverse proxy server can help offload some of the work from the HTTP server—like serving static content.

Nginx is a high-performance web server mainly used as a reverse proxy, load balancer, or HTTP cache. To install and run Nginx on a Linux distro running Ubuntu 16.04, run the following command on the server:

```
$ sudo apt-get update && apt-get install nginx
$ sudo service nginx start
```

Now if we open a browser and go to the remote address of the server, we should see the default Nginx page, as shown in Figure 11-4.

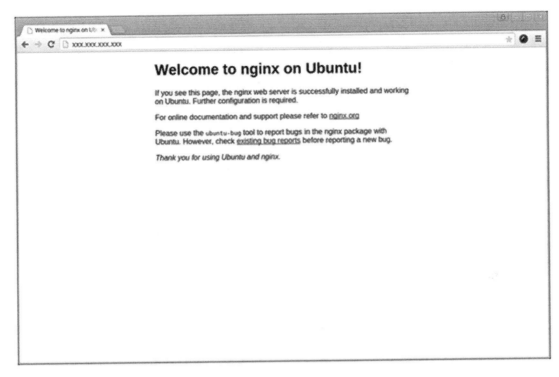

Figure 11-4. *The default page of a server running Nginx*

We are now ready to configure Nginx to serve our application. From a shell window on the remote server, open the *default* configuration file of Nginx in the *Nano* editor by executing the following command:

```
$ sudo nano /etc/nginx/sites-available/default
```

Replace the contents of the *default* file with the following:

```
server {
  listen 80;
  location / {
    proxy_pass http://localhost:5000;
    proxy_http_version 1.1;
    proxy_set_header Upgrade $http_upgrade;
    proxy_set_header Connection keep-alive;
    proxy_set_header Host $host;
    proxy_cache_bypass $http_upgrade;
  }
}
```

The preceding configuration tells Nginx to relay requests from port 5000 to port 80 and to set the relevant request headers. To save and exit Nano, press *Ctrl+O* and *Ctrl+X*, respectively.

Now when we send a request to the remote server by invoking the endpoint `http://<Remote IP>/ping`, we will see the response of "*Pong*" as expected, as shown in Figure 11-5.

Figure 11-5. *The result of a sample application running behind Nginx*

Hosting on Docker

ASP.NET Core applications can also be hosted and run inside a Docker container. If you're not familiar with Docker, it is the technology for providing the containerization of applications to allow them to run in an isolated environment on any platform that supports Docker.

Note   This section covers the basics of deploying an ASP.NET Core application to a Docker container, which is then compiled into a Docker image. It is an assumption that you have a basic understanding of what Docker is and how it works, and therefore further details will not be covered in this section. For more information on Docker, you can visit `https://docs.docker.com`.

To fully understand how to create a Docker image of our application and deploy it to a Docker container, we will go through the necessary steps, which include the bare minimum for running ASP.NET Core applications inside Docker.

Using the same sample application as we did in the first section, navigate to the root directory of the project and create a new file called Dockerfile, without any extension, that contains the following:

```
FROM microsoft/aspnetcore:2.0
WORKDIR /app
COPY /publish .
ENTRYPOINT ["dotnet", "AwesomeApi.dll"]
```

The contents of the Dockerfile build on the Microsoft/aspnetcore image with version 2.0. When it is executed, it copies the contents of the /publish directory to the current working directory, which is /app inside the container, and calls dotnet AwesomeApi.dll to run when the image executes.

The next step is to make sure that the /publish directory is created and populated with the published application. We do this by executing the following on the root directory of the project in a shell window:

```
$ dotnet publish -o ./publish
```

We specify the -o option on the dotnet publish command to indicate the output directory of the published artifacts.

We are now ready to build a Docker image for our application. From the root directory in a shell window, execute the following, which will build a new Docker image with the tag awesomeapi from the Dockerfile in the current directory:

```
$ docker build -t awesomeapi .
```

The Docker image is now ready to be used. To run the image inside Docker, we run the following command, specifying the name of the image as well as the name of the container as awesome:

```
$ docker run -d -p 8080:80 --rm --name awesomecontainer awesomeapi
```

The preceding command runs the awesomeapi image inside the awesomecontainer container in detached mode, meaning in the background, and maps all requests made to port 8080 to the internal port 80. The --rm option will ensure the container is stopped when the host exists. When we request http://localhost:8080/ping, it will invoke the application running inside Docker and return the expected "*Pong*" response.

Note   If you're using Docker for Windows and have not yet updated to the Windows Creators Update, there is a bug in how Windows communicates with Docker containers via *Network Address Translation* (NAT). At the time when this chapter was authored, you needed to access the IP address of the container directly, instead of localhost. To get the running container's IP address, execute the following from a shell window:

```
$ docker exec awesomecontainer ipconfig
```

It is a bit tedious having to call dotnet publish each time we want to create a Docker image of our application in order to have the latest bits included in the package. A recent update to Docker, however, made it possible to combine multiple steps in one Dockerfile.

Let's make some changes to our original Dockerfile:

```
FROM microsoft/dotnet:2.0-sdk
WORKDIR /app
COPY . ./
RUN dotnet publish -o out
ENTRYPOINT ["dotnet", "out/AwesomeApi.dll"]
```

Instead of using the microsoft/aspnetcore:2.0 image, we are now using the microsoft/dotnet:2.0-sdk image to initiate a build stage base for the rest of the instructions. Microsoft offers a variety of different flavors of .NET to address specific scenarios.

The microsoft/dotnet:<version>-sdk image contains the .NET SDK and includes .NET Core as well as the .NET Core CLI Tools and is to be used in the development of build scenarios. The microsoft/dotnet:<version>-runtime contains the .NET Core runtime and is optimized for production environments.

As we notice in the Dockerfile, all the files are copied to the working directory /app, and then executes `dotnet publish` to restore their dependencies and build and package the application to the /out directory.

One of the nifty features of Visual Studio 2017 is native support for *Dockerizing* .NET Core applications by using *Visual Studio Tools for Docker*. If you have the .NET Core cross-platform development workload installed from the Visual Studio 2017 installer, you are all good to go.

Docker support for .NET Core applications can be added for new or existing projects. When creating a new .NET Core application, just select the *Enable Docker Support* checkbox on the New ASP.NET Core Web Application dialog, as shown in Figure 11-6.

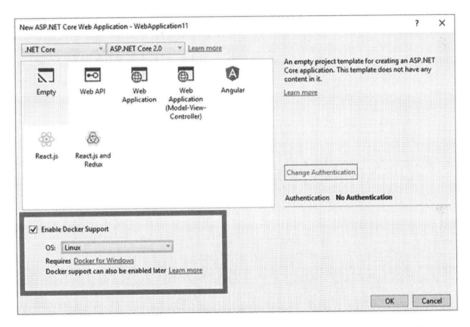

Figure 11-6. *Enable Docker support when creating a new ASP.NET Core application*

If you have an existing ASP.NET Core application, merely right-click on the project, point to *Add*, and then select *Docker Support*, as shown in Figure 11-7.

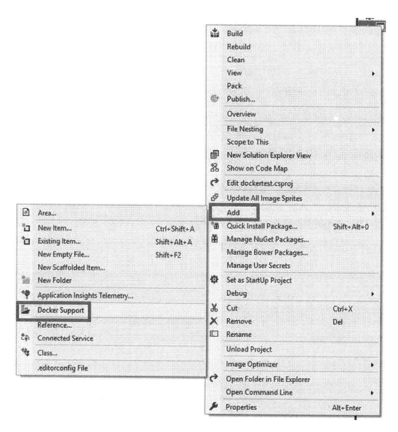

Figure 11-7. *Adding Docker support on existing ASP.NET Core applications*

Doing one of the preceding steps will add the required files and configuration to have the application run in Docker in no time. You will also notice that Visual Studio makes it possible to run and debug the application right from within Visual Studio. You do this by clicking the Docker *Run* button, which is available when selecting the *docker-compose* project as the default start-up project for the solution.

Note   When Docker support is added, Visual Studio adds an additional project called *docker-compose* to the solution, which contains Docker-specific files.

Publishing to Azure

Microsoft Azure is a cloud computing platform provided by Microsoft with which to build, test, deploy, and manage applications and services using a wide range of available offerings. One of those offerings is Azure App Service, a Platform-as-a-Service for creating and managing enterprise-grade, cloud-centric applications that can scale.

Let's use the same example as we did in the first section when we published our application to IIS, but this time we are going to the cloud using Azure App Service.

Note   To be able to create web applications in Azure for production purposes, you will need to have an Azure subscription. You can get a free trial here: `https://azure.microsoft.com/en-us/free`. Or, try Azure App Service without a subscription for a limited time by going here: `https://azure.microsoft.com/en-us/try/app-service/web`.

Like with the IIS scenario we covered earlier in this chapter, we need to create a logical web app first and then publish our application to it. Among the more natural ways of creating a web app in Azure is by using the Azure Portal, but this requires an Azure subscription, so we will make use of their offer for using Azure App Service for a limited time just to showcase how we deploy an ASP.NET Core application to Azure.

When navigating to `https://azure.microsoft.com/en-us/try/app-service/web`, we will be prompted to select an application type, and as Figure 11-8 shows, we need to choose *Web App* and click *Next*.

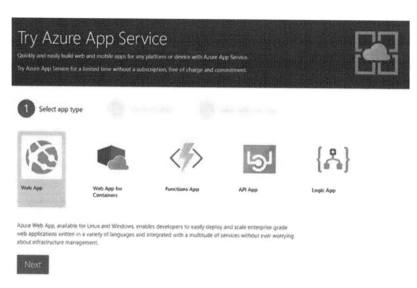

Figure 11-8. *Try Azure App Service: Select app type*

Going to the next step prompts us to select a template for the web app, as shown in Figure 11-9. Select *ASP.NET Core* and click *Create*.

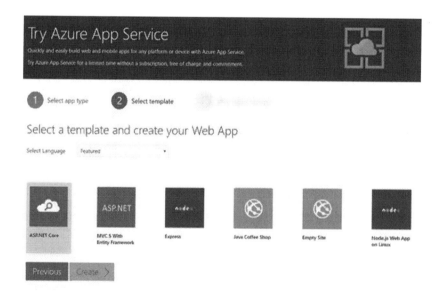

Figure 11-9. *Try Azure App Service: Select web app template*

After signing in with the provider of our choice, we are presented with a menu detailing ways of working with the Azure web app we've just created, as seen in Figure 11-10.

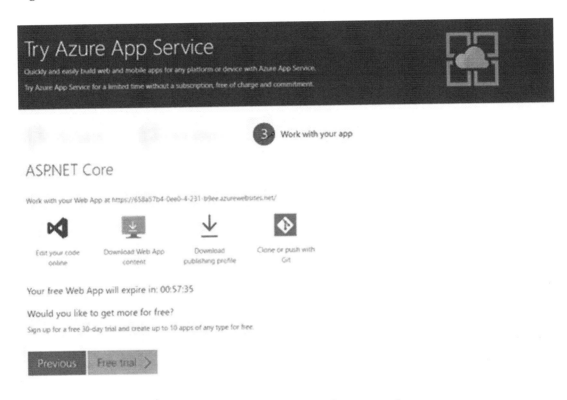

Figure 11-10. *Try Azure App Service: Work with your web app*

Here, we can edit the code online, download the web app content, download the publish profile, or use *Git* to clone and push changes. Download the publish profile by clicking *Download Publish Profile*. A publish profile is a file containing all the settings for deploying to a particular website.

Make a note of the generated web app URL. It is only valid for an hour before it expires, as it is only intended for experimental purposes only.

Back in Visual Studio 2017, with the sample project open, right-click on the project and select *Publish*. Doing so will open the Publish section of the project, as seen in Figure 11-11.

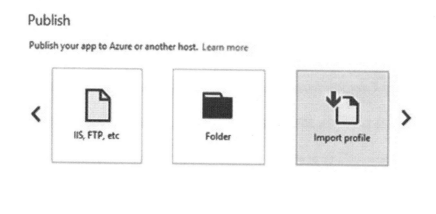

Figure 11-11. *The publish section of the project*

Scroll all the way to the right, select *Import profile*, then click *Publish* and select the publish profile downloaded earlier from Azure.

Note   If you have an Azure subscription, you could also publish directly to Azure from this menu by clicking the Microsoft Azure App Service item.

After you choose the publish profile, Visual Studio will proceed to publish the application to the web app configured in the publish profile. The publish profile is also added to the project to be used in the future.

When the publishing process is done, we can request the /ping endpoint in our newly deployed Azure web app:

```
http://e78c1c6d-0ee0-4-231-b9ee.azurewebsites.net/ping
```

Continuous Integration & Deployment

As mentioned before, the ultimate goal of any application is to run in a production environment. To help with automating things like getting changes from the developer's machine into source control, building and testing, and then finally deploying to an environment, we can make use of *continuous integration* (CI) and *continuous deployment* (CD).

Continuous integration is the process of merging all developer working copies into a shared branch that can be built to verify its quality. Continuous delivery is the process of automatically delivering the merged compiled code to a particular environment for use.

Visual Studio Team Services (VSTS) provides a platform for creating CI and CD pipelines to automatically deliver ASP.NET Core applications to the host of your choice, like Microsoft Azure, for instance. Figure 11-12 shows a diagram that explains the process of getting code into source control, built, and deployed to Azure using VSTS.

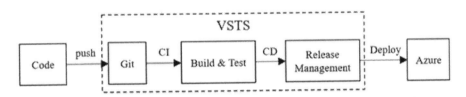

Figure 11-12. *The process of code to Azure using VSTS*

Note   To follow along with this tutorial, you will need to have a VSTS account and Azure subscription. Get a free VSTS account by going to `https://go.microsoft.com/fwlink/?LinkId=307137`.

In the previous section, we used the limited free offer from Microsoft Azure to create a web app. In this section, we will be building a web app using the Azure Portal.

After signing into the Azure Portal, click *New*, select *Web+Mobile*, and then click *Web App*, as shown in Figure 11-13.

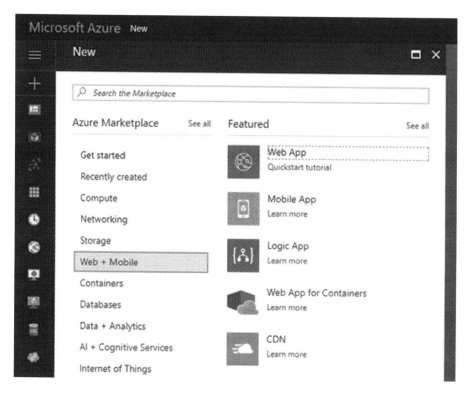

Figure 11-13. *Creating a new web app in Azure*

On the next screen, we will be prompted to fill in details about the web app. Here, we need to give the web app a name, choose the relevant subscription to run in, provide or create a new resource group as well as app service, and then click *Create*. Figure 11-14 shows an example web app being built.

Figure 11-14. *An example web app being created*

When Azure has finished provisioning the new web app, we can open the resource by clicking on its name under the *All Resources* section. We are now ready to configure continuous delivery on the web app, which we do by selecting the *Continuous Delivery* section and then clicking *Configure*, as shown in Figure 11-15.

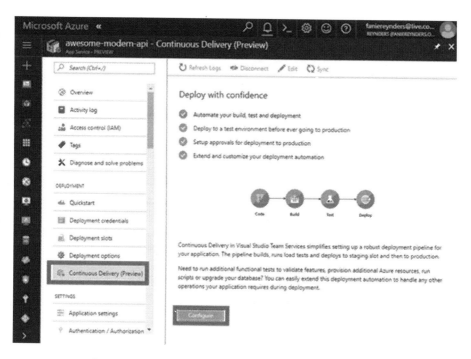

Figure 11-15. *Configure CD for Azure web app*

For the next step, the assumption is that we already have a configured VSTS account with a team project. On the *Configure Continuous Delivery* screen, set the source code provider as VSTS, as shown in Figure 11-16, and click *OK*.

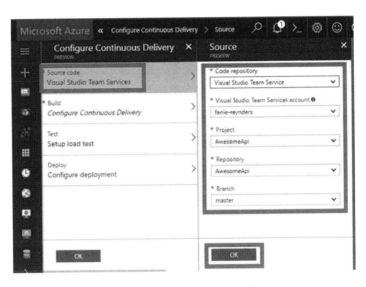

Figure 11-16. *Configure source code provider*

Under the *Build* section, select *ASP.NET Core* as the application framework, seen in Figure 11-17, and click *OK*.

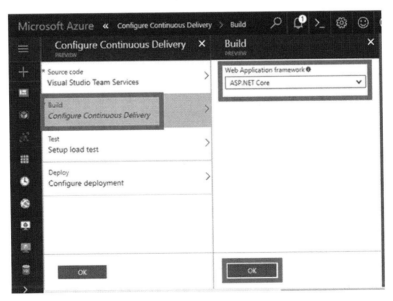

Figure 11-17. *Configure application framework for the build*

The last two sections, *Test* and *Deploy*, are considered out of scope for this example, so we will proceed by accepting the provided defaults and clicking *OK*.

After a short while, we have a configured CD pipeline and are presented with a screen like that shown in Figure 11-18.

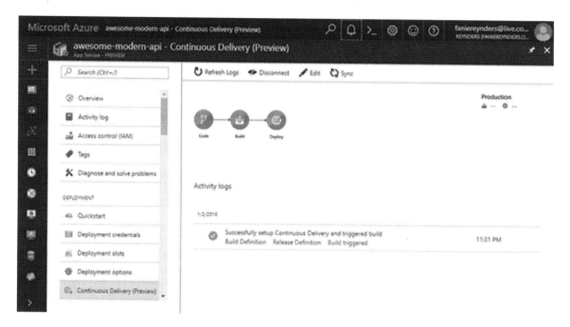

Figure 11-18. *The CD pipeline log*

We can click *Refresh Logs* to see the activity that happens on the CI/CD pipeline of the web app. The last thing to do is push our Awesome API, containing the /ping endpoint, to source control in VSTS.

From the root directory in a shell window, we execute the following command to initiate a local Git repository:

```
git init
```

Next, we need to connect the local Git repository to a remote on VSTS, and executing the following command does precisely that:

```
$ git remote add origin <VSTS Repository URL>
```

Now that the remote is connected, let's do a pull to get the latest version of the master branch:

```
$ git pull origin master
```

After the most recent version is pulled down, we need to add the local files to the repository, commit, and push the changes to the remote:

```
$ git add .
$ git commit -m "Yay! First commit"
$ git push
```

After our changes are pushed, we can go back to the CD activity log of the web app in Azure, sit back, and watch our application get published to the production environment.

Tip   If the build succeeds, but the release fails with the message *"no package found with specified pattern azure,"* then it is likely that there is no `web.config` or `wwwroot` folder included as part of the project. The default configuration we have followed automatically sets an option to look for web-based applications, and this requires either the `web.config` file or `wwwroot` folder to be present. You can either add these artifacts to the repository or un-check the option in VSTS.

Wrapping Up

We've come to the end of yet another chapter, and also ended this book with a bang. Looking back, this chapter was all about hosting and deploying ASP.NET Core applications to a variety of hosts in many different ways.

We've seen how to host an ASP.NET Core application on Windows by using IIS or as a Windows Service, and then jumped right into Linux-world by deploying an ASP.NET Core application running seamlessly with Nginx on Ubuntu. We briefly covered the basics of Docker and how to host ASP.NET Core applications in Docker containers, then ended the chapter by publishing our application to the cloud in Azure, complete with a configured CI/CD pipeline, which automatically deploys any changes made in the code to the production environment.

Index

A

© Fanie Reynders 2018
F. Reynders, *Modern API Design with ASP.NET Core 2*, https://doi.org/10.1007/978-1-4842-3519-5

Get the eBook for only $5!

Why limit yourself?

With most of our titles available in both PDF and ePUB format, you can access your content wherever and however you wish—on your PC, phone, tablet, or reader.

Since you've purchased this print book, we are happy to offer you the eBook for just $5.

To learn more, go to http://www.apress.com/companion or contact support@apress.com.

Apress®

Made in the USA
Lexington, KY
07 June 2018